Abstracts and Abstracting

CHANDOS
INFORMATION PROFESSIONAL SERIES

Series Editor: Ruth Rikowski
(email: Rikowskigr@aol.com)

Chandos' new series of books are aimed at the busy information professional. They have been specially commissioned to provide the reader with an authoritative view of current thinking. They are designed to provide easy-to-read and (most importantly) practical coverage of topics that are of interest to librarians and other information professionals. If you would like a full listing of current and forthcoming titles, please visit our website www.chandospublishing.com or email info@chandospublishing.com or telephone +44 (0) 1223 891358.

New authors: we are always pleased to receive ideas for new titles; if you would like to write a book for Chandos, please contact Dr Glyn Jones on email gjones@chandospublishing.com or telephone number +44 (0) 1993 848726.

Bulk orders: some organisations buy a number of copies of our books. If you are interested in doing this, we would be pleased to discuss a discount. Please email info@chandospublishing.com or telephone +44(0) 1223 891358.

Abstracts and Abstracting

A genre and set of skills for the twenty-first century

TIBOR KOLTAY

Chandos Publishing
Oxford • Cambridge • New Delhi

Chandos Publishing
TBAC Business Centre
Avenue 4
Station Lane
Witney
Oxford OX28 4BN
UK
Tel: +44 (0) 1993 848726
Email: info@chandospublishing.com
www.chandospublishing.com

Chandos Publishing is an imprint of Woodhead Publishing Limited

Woodhead Publishing Limited
Abington Hall
Granta Park
Great Abington
Cambridge CB21 6AH
UK
www.woodheadpublishing.com

First published in 2010

ISBN:
978 1 84334 517 6

British Library Cataloguing-in-Publication Data.
A catalogue record for this book is available from the British Library.

Typeset by Domex e-Data Pvt. Ltd.
Printed in the UK and USA.

Contents

About the author

Professor Tibor Koltay is Head of Department and Course
Director for Library and Information Science (LIS) curricula
at the Department of Information and Library Studies,
Faculty of Applied and Professional Arts, Szent István
University, Jászberény, Hungary. He also teaches at the
Department of Library and Information Science at the
University of West Hungary in Szombathely, Hungary.

Professor Koltay graduated from Eötvös Loránd University,
Budapest, Hungary in 1984 with an MA in Russian, and
gained his PhD there in 2002. In 1992 he was awarded the
Certificate of Advanced Studies in Library and Information
Science at Kent State University, Kent, Ohio, USA.

An experienced abstractor having written over 200
abstracts, Professor Koltay has been teaching abstracting
since 1992 and in 2003 published a Hungarian language
monograph on the theory and practice of abstracting.

The author may be contacted via the publishers.

Introduction

Abstracts and abstracting have a long history and the issues involved are still the subject of much comment, debate and research. Despite their changing role in the digital world, abstracts remain popular, even in cases where the user has complete full-text access, because the proper use of abstracts shields the searcher from unacceptable levels of irrelevance that result from full-text searching. In the changing information environment of our century and the era of Web 2.0, abstracting can be considered a fixed point characterised by the constancy, persistence and continuity of its values, yet still subject to development.

Much has been written about abstracts and abstracting. Although there is a relatively large number of textbooks on the topic, there is no up-to-date book on abstracting in English. As well as giving a comprehensive coverage of the topic, the aim of this book is to present a novel viewpoint, especially on informative and indicative abstracts. The discussion is based on an interdisciplinary approach, blending the methods of library and information science and linguistics. Thus the book strives to be a synthesis of theory and practice based on a large existing body of knowledge, which nonetheless is often characterised by misleading terminology and flawed beliefs.

This book is about abstracts and abstracting, a genre and a process that go together with a set of skills. Abstracts and abstracting may be called requisites of the twenty-first century with good reason. To discuss these issues thoroughly, a reflection on other, related genres is also necessary and will be provided.

Who is this book for?

This book is intended for three main groups of readers:

- professional abstractors (usually information professionals);
- researchers, who publish articles in scholarly journals;
- linguists and language teachers.

Information professionals work under different names and have different duties, but the majority of them learn about abstracts and abstracting. Many of them also write abstracts on papers that have appeared in scholarly and professional journals. (In our subsequent discussions we will use the words *article* and *paper* as synonyms.) From among librarians, reference librarians (mainly working in academic and special libraries) will most probably face the challenge of abstracting (Palais, 1988). There is one important category of information professionals, called information brokers, who usually work independently. For them abstracting is also an important skill and occupation (Rosen, 1988).

Researchers who publish papers in the scholarly journals of the fields of knowledge in which they work are usually required to write abstracts of their own papers. These are called *author abstracts*. We will define them in Chapter 2 on definitions and discuss their attributes in a subsection of Chapter 3.

Abstracting is also of interest to linguists and language teachers, especially practitioners who specialise in English for Specific Purposes (ESP) and English for Academic Purposes

(EAP), as well as English as a Second Language (ESL) and English as a Foreign Language (EFL), who can thus also make use of this book. Similarly, those who teach technical writing can find many parts of the book useful. At the end of this introduction, we will discuss this in more detail.

What is abstracting and what is an abstract?

Stated very simply, abstracting is the process of producing abstracts. It is a writing activity that allows information to be passed on in an economical way (Werlich, 1988).

To make the notion of the abstract clear, let us first take a simple, practice-oriented definition which states 'an abstract is a condensed version of a longer piece of writing that highlights the major points covered, concisely describes the content and scope of the writing, and reviews the writing's contents in abbreviated form' (Kilborn, 1998).

Although the word *abstract* can have different meanings in different contexts, it is usually assumed that an abstract will present the main contents of an original document. There is clearly a burning question: how can we identify this main or, in other words, most important content? It is the goal of this book to answer this question and in Chapter 5 we will concentrate in particular on doing so.

The abstract is a condensed document shorter than the original, the content of which is represented by the abstract. An abstract is a representation in the sense that it stands for another text (Cross and Oppenheim, 2006). We will develop this thought further in Chapter 2 on definitions.

Note: Up to this point we have been using – and will henceforth continue to use – the words *information* and *document* as near synonyms, even though we know, for example, that documents can also be regarded as containers of information. There are other similar cases which we will point out as necessary.

Why abstracts and abstracting?

In advertising its courses on abstracting, the Association for Information Management (Aslib, a professional organisation based in the United Kingdom) states the following:

> Information overload affects everyone, and there is an urgent need for people who can extract the key facts and opinions from documents rapidly and reproduce them accurately. Abstracting and summarising techniques are essential for current awareness services, enquiry answering and desk research, preparing briefings and writing reports. (Aslib, 2008)

This passage shows that many different types of abstracting can be found in libraries, information centres and other institutions concerned with information, as well as in the field of scientific and scholarly research. (Despite the slight but perceptible difference between the meaning of the words *scientific* and *scholarly*, we will use them interchangeably.)

There are, obviously, other different incentives to study abstracting and acquire abstracting skills. To explain the different motivations to write abstracts, we need to take a look at the nature of scholarly literature. Both information professionals and researchers of different disciplines know that there has been and still is an enormous growth in scholarly literature. This growth is especially notable in the (hard, natural) sciences, where researchers use scholarly journals both for publishing and gaining knowledge. The vast quantities of literature generally and of journal papers in particular make it extremely difficult to survey, find and use relevant publications. This has resulted in a demand for representations of documents that are not only condensed but are accurate and thorough. These representations – abstracts – have become the standard tools for accessing professional and scholarly literature (Pinto and Lancaster, 1999; Cross and Oppenheim, 2006).

As Lancaster (2003) points out, the growth in the quantity of information caused by the development of the Internet and especially the widespread use of the World Wide Web has made the situation even more complicated. If we regard the Internet as an information source, its main problem is not merely its size giving access to a tremendous quantity of information. The major problem is the lack of quality control. To be exact, there is no quality control that is similar or comparable to those mechanisms which characterise the information systems of the print environment. In the print environment, various institutions perform a quality filtering function. To begin with, publishers of scholarly books and journals apply a review procedure. In the case of journal papers, filtering is done by editors as well as by representatives of the given field's wider community. The latter perform a peer review to ensure that papers correspond to the norms of the field and are acceptable for the given scholarly community.

At the next level, indexing and abstracting services provide a quality filter in terms of the choices they make to index or abstract from among the published papers. Indexing services produce indexes of the literature. These contain not only bibliographic data such as the author, the title of the article, the name, the publication year, the volume and issue of the journal and the pages where a given paper appeared, but there is information about the topics covered by the papers. Abstracting services supplement these indexes with abstracts. Nowadays both services usually provide access to their products by means of databases.

Libraries, at the other end of the line, acquire only a selection of published materials. This produces a strong filtering system, the maintenance of which is important not only in the print environment but in the electronic, digital one as well (Lancaster, 2003).

The print environment, however, is not the only form of access to literature. Today it is economically feasible to store vast quantities of text in computer-searchable form, and the provision of such services allows libraries and scholars complete full-text access to a growing number of journal articles (Pinto and Lancaster, 1999). Nevertheless, this has not made abstracts redundant. Several authors argue that this is so. Pinto et al. (2008a) state that abstracts are still useful, for example because the development of the Internet has created a growing need for a variety of ways to filter information. Nicholas et al. (2007) argue that abstracts play a key role in helping scholars to deal with the digital flood, while Jacsó (2002) points out that the increasing availability of full-text databases has decreased the importance of abstracting and indexing databases but not the need for abstracts. The efficient use of full-text databases requires abstracts because they are extremely helpful in selecting the most promising source documents. If we limit a search in a full-text database to the abstract field, the results will be much more precise than searching large quantities of full-text documents. Pinto and Lancaster (1999: 234) put this as follows:

> On the surface, one might assume that knowledge discovery operations would be most likely to succeed when the complete text of items is processed. This is not necessarily so because full text can generate so

many spurious relationships that significant and useful associations will be virtually impossible to recognize. Abstracts may still have great value in knowledge discovery activities as they do in many others.

On the other hand, while the necessity and usefulness of abstracting has been questioned on several occasions, abstracts continue to be important for scholarly readers and abstracting remains a core scholarly service (Tenopir, 2008), because abstracts are powerful, complex and sophisticated tools which can be used to find relevant information (Pinto, 2006a). The reason for this is that in modern electronic (digital) library environments which make full text available on the Internet, the notion of metadata has become of special importance. Metadata (data about data) facilitate identification of digital documents and their retrieval. There are, at least, two types of metadata. Simple metadata could be useful for the location of resources, while richer metadata serve to aid selection – and abstracts are a basic component of the latter, richer type (Pinto, 2003a).

Why is searching abstracts more effective and more cost-efficient than the searching of full text? The reason for this is that the searching of full text often results in an unacceptable level of irrelevance (Pinto and Lancaster, 1999). From a different viewpoint we can say that the increase in the speed of accessing information has significant effects on writing and disseminating information that raises the importance of abstracts as tools for the transfer of information (Chan and Foo, 2004).

Abstracts and abstracting do indeed appear to have a future. Nicholas et al. (2007) jokingly report that some publishers recognise the key role of abstracts by suggesting that perhaps they should charge not for full texts but for abstracts. Joking aside, however, we need to understand that abstracts are typically free to view for all users while to view the full text of articles requires subscription. This means that some users can only view the abstracts as they have no other choice. Moreover, in some digital libraries abstracts have to be viewed before you can see the full text itself (Nicholas et al., 2007).

So how did abstracts and abstracting develop? Abstracts were originally designed to be read by humans and were very much tied to the papers published in scholarly journals. With the development of online information retrieval in the 1960s, abstracts became output from electronic databases, though they remained designed to be read by humans. So, if we think back to our consideration of the motivation to write abstracts, we can see that the reasons why researchers provide author abstracts are rather self-evident: they need to write abstracts if they want their articles to be published and read.

If we consider the most recent developments in the world of information, it is useful to pay attention to the arguments of Tenopir (2008), who warns us that every organisation committed to provide high-quality, authoritative information is challenged by the fact that in the new information environment user-generated content can coexist with authoritative content.

What, then, is this new information environment? The Web seems to have developed into a global forum for conversation (including written conversation), and with the explosive growth of online publishing the number of writers is on the increase (Beeson, 2005). In this environment writers have to realise that they are reaching a wide and varied audience which comprises specialists and non-professionals (Chan and Foo, 2004). In this context tools used for categorising documents fit well into the prevailing philosophy which characterises this environment and which is often called Web 2.0. Examples of such tools are folksonomies and tagging, which are gaining momentum in this environment. Folksonomies appear when (often lay) users add tags (keywords) to describe items on a website. For this they choose their own tags, and there are practically no restrictions or limitations on which keywords to chose, nor are there any existing controlled vocabularies or strict taxonomies to use either (Neal, 2007).

In our opinion, however, the above threat, brought about by the possibility of mixing authoritative content and metadata with user-added content and tags, is more real for indexing and cataloguing. There seems to be a lesser threat to abstracting, if any threat at all, and it may be not substantial even in the case of indexing and cataloguing. In this regard we can cite the opinion of Crawford (2009) who – speaking about academic libraries – points out that they will continue to benefit from professional indexing and abstracting as – despite the power of folksonomies and full-text retrieval – there is still a place for the professional organisation of information.

Abstracting, on the whole then, can still be described by the following statement:

> The focus must be on global information exchange, and scientists do not have time to read all the documents relevant to their research. These principles are as true today as they were 100 years ago. (Hawkins and Brynko, 2008: 27)

Beyond the usefulness of abstracts

Abstracting is a complex activity that employs information decoding and encoding. It develops critical reading skills and enhances the understanding of basic rhetorical principles, as it requires a thorough study of texts (Guinn, 1979). Nor can it be disputed either that abstracting promotes careful reading, summarisation and synthesising of information (Curtis and Bernhardt, 1992). And last but not least, abstracting is one of the higher-level activities of information literacy, an issue that we will address in more detail in Chapter 4.

While reading this, you may have noticed something peculiar: the words *abstract* and *summary*, *abstracting* and *summarisation*, respectively, have been used side by side. One of the reasons for this is that researchers in the field of computing speak about summarisation, as do linguists often as well. We will clarify the differences between abstracts and summaries in Chapter 2. Here we want to add only that summarising often has a wider meaning than abstracting. We will consider the issue further in Chapter 4 while the usefulness of abstracts will be discussed in Chapter 3.

Why don't we produce abstracts by computer?

Despite ongoing efforts, the production of abstracts by fully automatic means seems to be out of reach. This is especially true if we agree with the idea that the ultimate goal of automatic abstracting is to produce abstracts that are comparable to those which are the result of human intellectual effort (Johnson, 1995). There are many experiments on automatic abstracting (summarisation) systems. They produce, however, relatively low-quality summaries which are not comparable to those produced by humans. As a consequence, automatically produced abstracts often have to be revised by humans before they can be utilised (Montesi and Urdiciain, 2005a; Orasan and Hasler, 2006).

We know that the most frequently used methods for automatic abstracting are mainly of a statistical nature.

However, even the most sophisticated automatic methods are far from satisfactory, because the cognitive skills needed for information processing are related to factors such as volition and emotion which are part of human nature (Pinto, 2003a). The problems of summary generation thus are quite distinct from the generic task of language generation. What makes this field so elusive is the fact that the summarisation of an article involves its interpretation in order to identify the most important facts in it, followed by the generation of a text that conveys those facts concisely (McKeown et al., 1995).

Instead of producing summaries fully by computer, computer-aided summarisation is much more promising (Craven, 1993). The latter requires human interaction, thus knowledge of abstracts and abstracting skills are still needed.

Despite all this, we can be sure that automatic abstracting will continue to improve. However, it will probably be a very long time before computers will be intelligent enough to completely replace humans in these activities, if indeed they ever will be (Lancaster, 2003).

The interest of ESP in abstracts

There are several scientific disciplines that contribute to the study of abstracting and especially summarisation. Besides library and information science (LIS) disciplines such as psychology, artificial intelligence, cognitive science and linguistics are also involved (Endres-Niggemeyer, 1998).

The importance of linguistic approaches to abstracting is underlined by the fact that in the nomenclature issued by UNESCO in 1988 library and information science is not mentioned. However, abstracting appears under code 5701.01 and is a subordinate of *57 Linguistics* and of *5701 Applied linguistics* (UNESCO, 1988).

As already mentioned, abstracts and abstracting are of interest for ESP (EAP) practitioners, even though this genre has not been as extensively studied as the research article. The linguistic study of abstracts is a growing field, motivated by the interest of linguists to understand the mechanisms which underlie these multifunctional texts (Lorés, 2004). As surveyed by Chan and Foo (2004: 102), the main objectives of such studies have been directed towards 'identifying and assessing language conventions and rhetorical structures of abstracts in various disciplines, and on drawing implications for improving classroom practice and helping second language learners'. Despite these differences, the perspectives of the two disciplines are not mutually exclusive. On the contrary, there are several areas where their concerns overlap or mirror each other. In other words, whatever the preferences and differences in approach, we can see that both aim at producing better abstracts (Chan and Foo, 2004).

Although they represent a slightly different perspective, the short online guides to abstracting must also be mentioned. There is a relatively large number of such guidelines. They are usually prepared for university students in the USA and are presented by writing centres or similar institutions associated with departments of English. These guides also often address abstracting from an ESL perspective and treat abstracting as a practical writing issue. Many of them can be useful for those who are interested in abstracting, even though the terminology used in some may differ from that used in this book.

A genre and skills for the twenty-first century

Abstracting has a long history. Most sources date the appearance of abstracting services to the publishing of the

Journal des Sçavans in 1665 (Cleveland and Cleveland, 1983). We have argued – hopefully in a convincing way – that abstracting and abstracts have not only a past, but also a future. In the subsection on the information literacy background of abstracting in Chapter 4 we will deliver more supporting arguments that abstracts represent a genre for the twenty-first century and abstracting is a complex of knowledge, abilities, skills and attitudes of the same value. With regard to the notion of genres, we will discuss them in Chapter 6.

General advice to the reader

The issues related to abstracting are highly interdisciplinary. This book tries not only to show interdisciplinary approaches, but aims to synthesise theoretical knowledge and practical skills related to abstracting. It is, however, sometimes difficult to separate theory from practice.

Depending on your goals, you can chose either a more practical path to follow through the book or read the book in its entirety as the more theoretical chapters could also be enlightening.

Advice to information professionals

Abstracting is of prime importance for the information profession, and library and information professionals are those who usually learn abstracting systematically. While their knowledge may be limited to knowing the concepts and types of abstracts, their skills can extend to an ability to write usable abstracts.

Whatever the extent of knowledge and skills, information professionals may study abstracting during their formal library and information science education. On top of this there is the possibility of studying the subject within a framework of continuing professional development which in some countries may become more formal. This book is intended to be relevant whatever the form of education. Information professionals are advised to read this book in its entirety and not skip over any of its content.

Advice to researchers writing journal papers

You can skip, if you like, the theoretical chapters of this book, or you can give less attention to some of their subsections, though we can't promise that it will always be easy to do this. Don't forget, on the other hand, that theoretical explanations are meant to lay a foundation for practice. They can therefore also be helpful to you.

Advice to linguists (ESP, ESL, EFL professionals)

Although we said above that abstracting is usually treated from the ESL perspective as a practical writing issue, we believe that it would be of benefit for you to read the entire book, thus getting an insight into the interdisciplinary nature of abstracting.

Interdisciplinary and cross-disciplinary approaches

Even though we were considering the interests of information professionals and linguists in abstracting separately, the two approaches converge. Information professionals study and highlight the key qualities of abstracts, while ESP professionals study and teach the language skills needed to develop these features (Chan and Foo, 2004). This book puts abstracting into an information literacy context. Information literacy itself is an interdisciplinary concept which is – in our opinion – of prime interest not only to information professionals but also to linguists engaged in ESP activities. This will become evident in Chapter 4.

There are a number of concepts in this book we will take as given and so will not define them. In general, we assume that the reader knows more about the world of information, or at least needs less explanation to be able to use this book meaningfully. However, we do take the interdisciplinary nature of our message into consideration, which is why we will try to define linguistic concepts more frequently.

The structure of the book

This book has eight substantive chapters of different lengths. The main content of the first two chapters is very simple, and this first introductory chapter is followed by a chapter on definitions.

Chapter 3 is considerably longer and discusses the characteristics of the abstract – the length, functions and types of abstract. The latter issue receives especial attention as we intend to present a holistic picture on informative, indicative and indicative-informative abstracts. It is in this chapter that we discuss the relationship between the different types of abstract and their function.

The subsection on the objectivity of the abstract addresses an issue that is also of great importance. One aspect of the discussion on objectivity revolves around the question of whether abstracts should be critical or not. To answer this question, we include the case of *Mathematical Reviews* (2008) which – despite the name – is an abstracting database that encourages the publication of critical abstracts. Notwithstanding this, other aspects of objectivity are also treated in this book.

The author abstract is also relevant to the discussion in Chapter 3. As the knowledge and skills related to this type of abstract are essential to a wide range of readers, we consider it in detail and include advice to writers of author abstracts and a discussion of the issues relating to structured abstracts.

Chapter 4 provides the answer to another question: 'What does an abstractor have to know?' This part of the work addresses the knowledge, skills, attitudes and competencies needed to become a good abstractor.

To get a deeper insight into the nature of abstracting, we outline some problems of everyday and semi-professional summarisation. It is particularly useful to give special attention to the questions of proficiency in summarisation because abstracts are created in the process of summarising.

The information literacy context of abstracting is also explained because it is the most modern and in many regards burning question for a wide circle, including all those who may be interested in abstracting. In light of this, a subsection discusses the relationship between information literacy and abstracting. This chapter concludes with a short subsection which deals with the teaching of abstracting.

Chapter 5 is about the practice of abstracting. In this chapter you will become acquainted with the terminological questions of abstracting. Possible structures of abstracts are also outlined. We give advice on what to leave out and what to include in a good abstract. We also discuss whether the abstract should be written in one or more paragraphs and what the sequence of information reflected in the abstract should be.

The subsection on types and techniques of reading is followed by thoughts on the language used in abstracts: the past tense and the third person, negation and negatives, the passive or active voice and the vocabulary.

Chapter 6 provides two examples of the creation of abstracts, showing the phases of analysis, editing and generating the final abstract. This chapter concludes with a short subsection about the evaluation of abstracts.

Chapter 7 bears the title 'Beyond language and style'. Were we to express the content of this chapter in the simplest way, we would say that it is about everything that we could not say in the previous chapters which is, nonetheless, of interest. The title of one of the subsections is telling: 'A genre in its own right'. It is in this chapter that we give insight into knowledge acquired about abstracting and comprehension, because comprehension is foundational to abstracting, provided that we take into consideration the differences that exist between 'normal' comprehension and comprehension directed towards abstracting.

Last but not least we address other related processes such as indexing and translation. The very last subsection throws light on some additional aspects of abstracting, and includes among others some models of the process. Finally, Chapter 8 recapitulates the main message of the book in a short form. The book also contains an index in which we indicate only those concepts that cannot be easily identified from the table of contents and do not figure in this introduction or the conclusion.

Definitions

Besides the obvious fact that a handbook like this requires all concepts to be defined thoroughly, there is a further reason to do so: the unruly and contradictory nature of terminology in this field. In the field of abstracting there are a number of ill-defined concepts and terms used in a contradictory and inconsistent manner. However, we do not want to spend an unduly long time and waste energy on discussing these terms. Rather we will use our best efforts to employ the terminology consistently, and to apply the terms we regard the most appropriate and which are accepted by the majority of sources.

The abstract

We can take the definition of Kilborn (1998) we provided in Chapter 1 as a starting point and develop it further. Employing more academic wording results in the following:

> *An abstract is a text that contains the most important content of an already existing text in a concise, condensed and abbreviated form.*

This definition can be developed further by making some qualifying remarks.

- The text the content of which is reflected on in the abstract is the primary or original text (often simply called 'the original').
- The primary text is longer than the abstract.
- Both texts are in a written form, fixed either on paper or any other non-paper (e.g. electronic, optical) storage media.
- Abstracts serve informing (informational) goals.

The ambiguity of the term 'abstract'

Before going further with the definition, we should add that the genre of the abstract is in fact an umbrella term covering three sub-genres. Following the line of thought of Gläser (1993) and Rothkegel (1995) we can describe these sub-genres as follows. In all three sub-genres there is a situational context: we have two different but related texts. One is an original document that fulfils the role of knowledge source. The other is a derived (secondary) text which is closely connected to the knowledge source. The knowledge source is relatively long – longer than the derived text. We will call the first a *maxi-text* and the second a *mini-text*.

There are three different scenarios:

1. Both texts are produced (more or less) at the same time and by the same author. The maxi-text is an article and the mini-text is called an 'author abstract'. The maxi-text is the knowledge source for the mini-text. In other words, the derived text is closely connected to the research article that has been written by the same author. It is not necessary that one of the texts pre-exists the other.

2. The maxi-text is available but the mini-text still has to be constructed. Consequently we are dealing with a pre-existing text and the task is to write an abstract.

This purported text, however, is not an author abstract but an abstract written by someone else who is not the author of the original maxi-text. In addition, here, the maxi-text is the knowledge source for the mini-text. The derived text is physically separated from the original to which it refers and we have separate authors for the article and for the abstract. The author of the latter is called an 'abstractor'. As a rule, abstracts of this type are published in abstracting journals or databases that contain abstracts. To give a full picture, we should say that author abstracts are also often included in abstracting journals and databases. This happens despite the fact that author abstracts have been historically more closely tied to journal articles.

3. The mini-text is constructed without any pre-existing maxi-text which will be produced later. This is the situation when we announce a paper, for example, at conferences. This time the mini-text is the knowledge source for the maxi-text. This has a very practical explanation. At a conference an abstract is required before a paper can be accepted. In this case we have a pre-text (an 'unfinished' or 'promissory text'), that is a text which will be elaborated into a full text, usually a conference paper. The pre-existing text is now the mini-text.

All this shows that the word *abstract* denotes an umbrella term which covers both author abstracts and abstracts whose authors differ from the authors of the original texts (Types 1 and 2). Type 3 is a concept that differs from the other two. It is almost a homonym. The difference lies in the fact that such promissory texts are usually prepared before the full paper. There is no original either in the sense of Type 1 (almost parallel processing) or as in the case of Type 2. The context of such conference abstracts depends both on the underlying research and on the type of discourse involved. The latter can be a plenary lecture, a workshop, a poster, etc. All these types require different conference papers (Montesi and Urdiciain, 2005a). Evidently, the processes that lead to the creation of conference abstracts show much similarity to those which generate abstracts depicted under Types 1 and 2. To begin with, they too reflect some content in an abbreviated form, even though that content does not yet exist in written form. Nonetheless, whatever the similarities and differences, we will not address the topic of conference abstracts since they represent a different genre.

As pointed out above, one of the main differences between author abstracts and abstracts written by professional abstractors is that the latter can be written in parallel with the original articles. In fact author abstracts are written usually after the body of the paper. December and Katz (1991) put this in the following way:

> Although an abstract appears as the first section of a paper, it should be written last. You need to have completed all other sections before you can select and summarize the essential information from those sections.

We have already seen that abstracts are derived text genres because they depend on previously existing primary, original texts. Primary text genres, on the other hand, are independent texts which are an original contribution to a specific subject area or province of discourse. These include research articles, monographs, essays, etc.

Derived text genres, then, are based on underlying primary texts. They depend on the subject matter and the concrete topic, the conceptual and terminological systems and the linguistic means of the primary texts. For the sake of completeness, we should also add that an aspect of derived genres not mentioned here pertains to oral communication (Gläser, 1993).

The textual nature of the abstract

We said above that abstracts are texts. What does this mean? First of all, we want to stress that they are not computer-produced quasi-texts which do not qualify as natural language (verbal) texts.

If abstracts are verbal texts, it is necessary to define this concept, and there are, plainly, plenty of definitions. In one of the perhaps best-known and widely accepted works on this subject, de Beaugrande and Dressler (2002) define text as a communicative occurrence which should meet seven standards of textuality:

1. *Cohesion* concerns the ways in which the components (the actual words) of the surface text are mutually connected within a sequence. This happens according to grammatical forms and conventions, thus surface sequences cannot be radically rearranged without causing disturbances.

2. *Coherence* concerns the ways in which the components of the textual world, concepts and relations are arranged in the text. Such arrangements can be causality or relations in time.

3. *Intentionality* concerns the attitude of the producer of the text towards producing cohesive and coherent texts.

4. *Acceptability* concerns the attitude of the receiver of the text that a cohesive and coherent text has some use for the receiver.

5. *Informativity* concerns the extent to which textual elements are expected or known.

6. *Situationality* concerns the factors which make a text appropriate in a particular situation.

7. *Intertextuality* (or context) concerns the factors which make the utilisation of one text dependent on knowledge of other (previously known) texts.

(The concepts of the 'deep structure' and 'surface structure' will be addressed in more detail in Chapter 7.)

As we have said above, abstracts are not only texts but are written texts. We have also said several times before that abstracts are secondary texts. This, however, does not mean that they are not self-contained. Being self-contained in the context of abstracting means that derived texts are understandable without reading (consulting) the primary text. In other words, they can stand alone. The mere fact that abstracts are natural-language texts means that they are self-contained. Notwithstanding this, we often find it stated in the literature on abstracting that abstracts are capable of standing alone (Carraway, 2007) and are intelligible to the reader without reference to the documents they represent (ANSI, 1997). Although it seems to be a kind of tautology, this statement is dictated by tradition and is directed more towards the conciseness of the abstract's content than to its textual nature.

The requirement that abstracts have to be self-contained and able to stand alone is, nonetheless, important. Recourse to the original has to be limited only to the acquisition of more detailed information. Provided the reader has some knowledge of the subject, it means that we can make sense of the abstract's message without having the original to hand (Lannon, 1990; Rowley, 1988).

The importance of a pre-defined viewpoint

As indicated earlier, abstracts are texts that contain the most important information in other, existing texts. We also know that abstracts have to be shorter than the original, primary texts. Here, however, we want to stress that abstracts serve informing (informational) goals. This requires some kind of pre-defined viewpoint on how the abstract reflects the most important information of the pre-existing original. We will discuss all these functions further in Chapter 3.

Abstracts vs. summaries

Abstracts may be contrasted with summaries in two different aspects. First of all, we can say that these two words are often mixed up, although they represent two different concepts. The American Standard on Abstracting clarifies this in the following way:

> A summary is a brief restatement within a document (usually at the end) of its salient findings and conclusions and is intended to complete the orientation of the reader who has studied the preceding text. Because other vital portions of the document (for example, purpose or methodology) are not usually condensed into this type of summary, the term should not be used synonymously with «abstract»; i.e. an abstract as defined above should not be called a summary. (ANSI, 1979: 7)

The soundness of this explanation is corroborated by the fact that this type of summary is often called a *concluding summary*. Concluding summaries follow sections of the text and summarise important points within them (Vaughan, 1991). In articles, there is usually only one concluding summary, at the end. Summaries can be a structural part of articles, although Carraway (2007) is of the opinion that summary sections are redundant as they repeat information provided in the author abstract. Including summaries in articles, nonetheless, seems to belong to the traditions of writing scientific articles.

On the other hand, the nouns *abstract* and *summary* and the corresponding verbs can be used as synonyms. To be exact, summaries represent a broader category than that of the abstract. In the introductory Chapter 1 of this book, and especially in the subsection on automatic abstracting, we have already spoken about summaries, and we should not forget that abstracts come into being in the process of summarisation. Summaries according to this definition are thus condensed representations of textual contents. We will consider them further in the subsection on professional summarisation in Chapter 4.

When speaking about summaries, there is one genre which merits our special attention. It is the *executive summary*, which we will come back to soon.

The full definition

The above discussion yields the following full definition of an abstract:

> *An abstract is a text that reflects the most important information of an existing (primary) text in a form shorter than the original. The importance of information is decided from a pre-defined viewpoint, which enables the abstract to serve informing (informational) goals.*

The types of abstracts

There are three types of abstracts:

- the indicative abstract;
- the informative abstract;
- the indicative-informative (mixed) abstract.

We will discuss these types further in Chapter 3. However, we should stress that these three types do not depend on who has produced the abstract. They can be either author abstracts or abstracts produced by professional abstractors.

The original

The concept of the original deserves special attention. As mentioned earlier, those texts which are abstracted are called *primary text*s or *original text*s, or sometimes simply *original*s. Although we will find a number of different approaches in the literature to the problem of originals, we wish to state that originals are articles published in scholarly or professional journals. This means that originals are written texts which report on developments and achievements in the natural (hard) sciences, the social sciences, the humanities or some other profession.

We have pointed out that author abstracts may be produced at more or less the same time as the originals and are written by the same authors. In this case it is almost self-explanatory that originals are journal papers.

In the case of abstracts written by someone different from the author of the original, there is a more complicated picture. In the literature on abstracting we often find other document types as possible originals. This is, however, much more a question of terminology and the different use of concepts, an issue that we will not discuss in detail here. In any case, we want to limit our discussion to abstracts the originals of which are journal articles. This is especially pertinent when we consider that the majority of abstracts reflect the content of journal articles.

While we are discussing journal articles, it is worth mentioning that they represent a genre of the scientific style. This style materialises in a number of scientific text types, all of which are designed to be deliberately logical and consistent. Their authors' intention is to present their main ideas in the best way possible. Scientific texts are usually constructed in a special way in which the main ideas are surrounded by sentences that serve as a kind of introduction and conclusion to a given fragment of the text (Emashova, 2008).

Related concepts and genres

A number of other related concepts and genres also need to be defined. Many of these definitions can easily be derived from the definition of an abstract or, we could say, naturally. To give a concise overview, nonetheless, requires that we define all possible concepts. However, while many of these definitions seem to be obvious or self-explanatory, not all of them are quite so clear-cut.

Abstracting, abstractor, author abstract

We have defined the abstract and touched upon the closely related concept of *abstracting* which we will now look at in more detail. Abstracting is the activity of representing the most important information of a text in a text that is shorter than the original from a pre-defined viewpoint. To put it simply, it is the writing of abstracts, including the writing of author abstracts and abstracts produced by someone who is not the author of the original text.

We also have to give attention to the concept of the *abstractor*. The abstractor is a person who produces abstracts. There are two main types of abstractor:

- authors of primary texts;
- professional abstractors.

Journal editors are also producers of abstracts (Staiger, 1965). Their role, however, is rather restricted as they edit abstracts provided by their authors. Theoretically it is possible for editors to write abstracts on behalf of those authors who did not produce them for some reason. This is, nonetheless, unusual, as professional and scholarly journals require authors to write abstracts for their papers. Nevertheless, if editors write abstracts, they are acting as professional abstractors.

What knowledge do abstractors need to have? What are the abilities, skills and attitudes they need? We will discuss this thoroughly in Chapter 4 which is dedicated to abstractors and their competencies.

The importance of *author abstract*s and the problems related to them will also be discussed in Chapter 4. Although we have already touched upon their nature, it is necessary, to define them briefly here. An author abstract is an abstract produced by the same author who produced the primary (original) text.

The annotation and the synopsis

The genre of the *annotation* is most often defined as a brief explanation of a document or its contents, usually added to the original text as a note to clarify its title (ANSI, 1997). This hardly differentiates it from an indicative abstract the nature of which will be discussed in Chapter 3. The clearest and most useful distinction, however, is to say that annotations reflect the content of books while abstracts – as defined earlier – reflect the most important content of journal articles (Koltay, 2003).

The word *synopsis* was formerly used to denote author abstracts with the aim of differentiating them from abstracts written by professional abstractors. This distinction, however, is now rarely made (ANSI, 1979; Rowley, 1988).

The extract

Aside from the summary, the first and perhaps most important related genre is the *extract*. This consists of portions (sentences) of the original text that have been copied verbatim and have been selected to represent the whole (ANSI, 1997). They show some limited usefulness but represent the original in a different way to abstracts, nor do they form cohesive wholes (Russel, 1988; Kittredge, 2002).

The executive summary

The genre of the *executive summary* is related to that of the abstract and deserves special attention. There are, however, significant differences between them. The target audience of executive summaries – as the name suggests – is the busy executive. The secondary audience is middle managers. Both categories are interested in bottom-line deliverables. They concentrate on decisions and not on methodologies and details. Executive summaries usually identify a need or problem and take the implications of that problem into consideration. They then give an inventory of solutions, recommend the preferred solution and explain its value, giving the key reasons. Just like abstracts they are self-contained, that is they are understandable without consulting the full document itself, and even more so than abstracts, executive summaries are read more often than the full documents which are sometimes not read at all. In contrast to abstracts which are characterised by a detached and neutral style, the tone of executive summaries is often persuasive (Clayton, 2006; Vaughan, 1991). There are other differences in addition. In the case of executive summaries, the original documents are not journal articles but proposals, reports and the like. In general, it is questionable if we can speak about original documents in the sense we did in the case of abstracts as executive summaries are almost inseparable and structural parts of their parent documents.

The characteristics of the abstract

Successful abstractors possess a thorough knowledge of the characteristics of abstracts. To facilitate this, in this chapter we are going to address the important properties that all abstracts have. The opening subsections consider the length, function and types of abstracts. We will see that these three issues are so deeply interrelated that the order in which they have been considered is almost irrelevant. After these, we will also discuss an important but somewhat different issue: the objectivity of the abstract. Finally, we address the issues related to the author abstract. It is often the subject of debate. As the knowledge and skills related to it are essential to a wide range of our readers, we give it suitable attention in the concluding subsection of this chapter.

The length

As explained in Chapter 2 on definitions, abstracts are supposed to be shorter than their originals. This shows that the length of the abstract is a question of prime interest. This issue is apparently seen and treated differently by different authors.

A simple and trivial definition of an abstract's length is that it has to be shorter than the original otherwise it is meaningless to produce one. This approach, nonetheless, is used rarely (Koltay, 2003).

A review of the literature by Armstrong and Wheatley (1998) points out that abstracting services often prefer short abstracts for the obvious reason that length affects production and storage costs, as well as printing, binding and distribution costs when paper copies are produced. However, their examination of the guidelines of eleven database producers revealed no accepted norm for abstract length. Recommendations varied from 'As brief as possible' to 'No limit' and from 50 to 500 words.

The idea of brevity also prevails in the digital era where physical limits seem to matter less. Apparently there are reasons of principle that direct the perception of this issue, for example that saving the user time remains a prime goal.

Several sources have advice on the matter of length. Day (1988), for example, votes for a maximum length of 250 words. The same measure is set in the 1997 ANSI standard. It adds, however, that the abstract's length should be appropriate to the potential usefulness of the document abstracted (ANSI, 1997). Waters (1982) is of the opinion that in abstracts shorter than 200 words important information may be missing, while abstracts over this limit could contain much redundant information. He adds, notwithstanding, that the original's length is decisive. Ashworth (1973) denies this and stresses that indicative and informative abstracts should be of different lengths. (We will provide a short explanation for this in the subsection on informative and indicative abstracts below.)

Similarly, Collison (1971) directs our attention to the fact that abstracts designed to be substitutes for the originals are longer than other abstracts. (With regard to substitution see the subsection on the functions of abstracts.) This is not the only question on which we can agree with Collison. He states that the desirable length should allow the inclusion of the most important information in the original. The length of the original is undoubtedly a factor which should not be neglected. When defining an abstract, we mentioned that the originals are articles published in scholarly or professional journals. A number of 'Instructions to Authors' provided by such journals limit the length of a scientific article to between 2,000 and 4,000 words. Abstracts represent the content of these and this length of the originals has a very strong influence on the length of the abstracts.

We often find that the desirable length of abstracts is expressed in percentages. Borko and Bernier (1995), for example, suggest that an abstract's length should be between 10 and 20 per cent of the original. Carraway (2007) sets the goal at 250 or fewer words, adding that it should be no more than 3 per cent of the original's length.

Stotesbury (2003) studied 300 author abstracts from the domain of the humanities, the social sciences and natural sciences. She found that the length of the abstracts varied from 20 to 560 words. The respective editorial policies of the journals, however, kept the length of the abstracts within a given journal fairly consistent. A sample of 27 abstracting databases studied by Armstrong and Wheatley (1998) showed an average length of 114 words, but this figure varied considerably, with the smallest average length at 19 words and the largest at 258 words.

All this shows that absolute standards are not applicable to abstract length. Instead, it is advisable to take several factors into consideration:

- the language of the original;
- the physical availability of the original;
- the length of the original;

- semantic features of the original (among others its complexity and the density of information in it);
- the importance of the original for the abstracting service;
- the practice followed by the abstracting service (whether it requires informative abstracts or limits the length, etc.). (Pinto, 1992; Pinto and Lancaster, 1999)

If we consider the implications of the above list, two closely associated factors become apparent: the original and the needs of the user community which are often represented by an abstracting service that acts on behalf of its potential and targeted users. If the original is long but its content is not particularly dense, the abstract will be relatively short, if there is an abstract at all.

On the other hand, if it is difficult to obtain the original and/or its language is unfamiliar to a number of users, a longer abstract can be provided (Collison, 1971).

The problem of length is much more simple in the case of author abstracts. The limits set by the journals have to be abided.

Last but not least, abstracts should correspond to the so-called 'bikini principle': they have to be large enough to cover all the important information, but small enough to be interesting to the reader (De Guire, 2006).

Functions

As an introduction to the functions of abstracts, let us state first that, generally speaking, the purpose of abstracting is to give an idea about the content of a text to someone who does not know that text. This is done without retelling every detail of the original (Werlich, 1988). Abstracts are a vital component of research communication as they can reach many times more readers than original articles (Staiger, 1965).

Abstracts are intended to meet a number of purposes, as, for example, expressed by Zellers et al. (2008):

> Readers use abstracts to see if a piece of writing interests them or relates to a topic they're working on. Rather than tracking down hundreds of articles, readers rely on abstracts to decide quickly if an article is pertinent. Equally important, readers use abstracts to help them gauge the sophistication or complexity of a piece of writing. If the abstract is too technical or too simplistic, readers know that the article will also be too technical or too simplistic.

Despite the complex nature of the objectives set for abstracts and abstracting it is necessary to classify their functions. The functions of an abstract may be understood in two ways:

- functions in the strict sense;
- additional 'benefits'.

Functions in the strict sense

The main functions of abstracts are expressed by Fidel (1993) who states that abstracts increase the efficiency of information gathering as they

- give orientation to users;
- provide an overview for those who need to keep up to date;
- serve as a source of information.

These goals are attained when the abstract fulfils one or more of the following functions:

- localisation;
- retrieval;
- substitution.

Before we discuss each individual function, it should be stated that these functions can be approached in a more balanced way if we say that abstracts are polyvalent. This means that they may answer different user demands, from the localisation of the original within a given collection to its substitution (Pinto, 2003b).

Abstracts save the reading time of individual researchers and improve the control of information (Hutchins, 1993). Time-saving is achieved by informing readers about the exact content of the original, indicating in this way whether the full text merits their further attention. This is possible, because abstracts present in a condensed way the macro-propositions of the original (Martín Martín, 2003). (For more on macro-propositions and macrostructures see the relevant subsection in Chapter 7 that explains some of the issues regarding comprehension.)

Localisation is a function that appeared first in abstracting history. This basic function continues to be an important one. Its essence is to give a signal about the existence of the original and help readers to decide if the original is likely to be of sufficient interest (Cross and Oppenheim, 2006). This is the reason why this function is also called the *signalising* function.

Based on these signals the user makes a decision about the need to consult the original (Staiger, 1965). In making this decision we can either ignore the original or examine it more carefully (Kuhlen, 1984). Any abstract, written by the author or by information professionals, whether indicative or informative, can fulfil localisation. This is the function that has belonged to abstracts from the early stages of their development. It continues to be their basic aim, in particular with respect to author abstracts that appear together with the text of the article. In these cases abstracts are inseparable structural parts of articles. This is true not only when they are physically integrated with the papers, but also when they appear in indexes and databases enriched with abstracts. This latter connectedness is much more contextual than physical.

The *retrieval function* builds on localisation but nonetheless goes beyond it. This function is to aid the assessment of document relevance (Cross and Oppenheim, 2006). The first step of information retrieval usually brings in a relatively high number of hits. This means simply that a large number of articles have been found in the search that may be of interest for the user.

The really relevant articles, however, can best be selected with the use of abstracts. They present much more information about the content of the original than bibliographic data, keywords and index terms (Cleveland and Cleveland, 1990; Cremmins, 1982; Rowley, 1988). Carraway (2007: 412) expresses this as follows:

> When conducting a literature search, researchers may read abstracts of perhaps 100s of papers in which the titles possibly have a bearing on an aspect of their work. Only if the content of the abstract seems relevant will researchers progress to reading the article from which the abstract was derived.

The role of abstracts in aiding retrieval received more emphasis with the appearance of databases. Print indexes often did not contain abstracts, while their electronic equivalents usually enable their use. In this case the retrieval function acquires even more importance than in a journal, as the abstract becomes a searchable field (Montesi and Urdiciain, 2005b).

While we are on the subject of the retrieval function, it is important to understand that there are two groups of retrospective searchers. The first group includes those who seek one or two items about a limited subject. They may also look for documents by a particular author or from a specific institution. Because such searchers have their own set of evaluation criteria, they carry out a mental evaluation of the search results during the search and for them abstracts may be of limited help. The second group, however, may be working on comprehensive assignments that involve large amounts of information on a subject with which they are less familiar. Such searches may involve literature spanning many years, even back to the beginning of literature on the given topic. In this case informative abstracts help to rule out less relevant references (Rowlett, 1985).

In Chapter 1 we mentioned that abstracts were originally designed to be read by humans. This still seems to be the case, even if they can also serve as searchable fields. However, they fulfil, without question, a much more important role when they are read in order to make decision about the relevance of a paper, as described above. We should add that a study by Fidel (1986) shows that the use of abstracts for free-text retrieval has been a relatively neglected field, although the 1997 ANSI standard also points out that abstracts facilitate free-text searching in an electronic environment (ANSI, 1997).

The next subsection of this chapter will consider the types of abstracts, but at this stage we want only to point out that not all types of abstracts are able to fulfil the retrieval function – only informative abstracts are able to do this.

Substitution is far from being accepted by everyone. On the contrary, it is subject to debate. The question here is self-evident: can the use of abstracts make the use of the original unnecessary? Can they be surrogates of the originals? From a purely theoretical viewpoint and in absolute terms, substitution is impossible as the original could be substituted only by itself in the light of the fact that abstracts by their very nature contain less information than originals. There are consequently many who deny the possibility of substitution. Rowlett (1985), for example, is of the opinion that abstracts are not surrogates as they are not designed to be the final source of precise and complete data.

The question of substitution is evidently much more complicated and it is possible to say yes under certain circumstances. Whatever the standpoint, it is important to take note that there is a need for abstracts that can substitute for the original because there is a set of users who require this, namely users who are lacking the command of a given (foreign) language or have limited time to read the professional literature. It is for this reason that we can speak of substitution at all. In the meantime, it is necessary to discuss its limitations, one of which lies in the relative nature of substitution. There is another limitation which is of a more or less ethical nature. It is about the fact that serious scholarship cannot be based on information gained from abstracts only. Researchers who want to keep up with the developments in their field have to use the full text of original articles. Original texts are the only acceptable sources of information for use directly in research and development. Researchers can, however, obtain these texts by making use of the retrieval function of abstracts.

On the other hand, it is important to differentiate between the main research topics of researchers and their additional, fringe interests. The latter require less information and a more superficial treatment, and there is less time to read the literature that deals with such topics. In this case researchers can often obtain enough information from an abstract to make the reading of the whole document unnecessary (ANSI, 1979).

The question of the lack of linguistic abilities is slightly different. Native speakers of English are in a fortunate situation as this language is usually sufficient to be able to follow the published record of science and be published internationally. Those whose mother tongue is not English have to decide whether to learn foreign languages other than English.

If researchers encounter articles that are of interest to them and available in a foreign language of which they do not have command, they can either ignore them or use abstracts to obtain part of the information they require. However, the problem of articles in 'rare' languages is often coupled with difficulties in obtaining the original full text itself.

Any or all of these difficulties in combination result in situations where using abstracts alone would not be unethical, provided that the abstracts give more explicit and detailed coverage of the content of the originals (Ashworth, 1973).

While we said that it is possible to carry through the retrieval function using informative abstracts, this is even more the case with substitution as it is informative abstracts that can act as surrogates. (See also the subsection on informative abstracts.)

Additional benefits

As said above, besides the functions in the strict sense, abstracts have other properties that are useful to their users. Most of these benefits reflect the possible inter-lingual nature of abstracting. For example, there is a possibility that the original and the abstract are written in different languages. In this way abstracts can make information published in a foreign language available (Fidel, 1993). In terms of foreign language use, abstracts help to overcome the language barrier if they are written in the user's own language or in a language that is more familiar to them than the language of the original (Cross and Oppenheim, 2006).

Some of the benefits come irrespective of the native language of an abstract's users. First of all, an abstract helps readers to understand the full text by acting as a pre-reading outline of the key points. Reading an abstract before reading an article helps readers anticipate what is coming in the text itself. The overview obtained in this way makes reading the text easier and more efficient (Zellers et al., 2008). Abstracts can also provide some language preparation for a given text by including key words and ideas that are found in the original which can serve as a key to understanding fully the argument of the original (Cross and Oppenheim, 2006).

A final group of additional benefits comes in the post-reading phase. These are related to reading articles both in someone's native language and in a foreign language. Even after reading the originals, readers often keep abstracts to remind them of supporting sources. In this role abstracts can help the reader to remember the content of the article and its given topic. As abstracts include complete bibliographic citations, sources are easily identifiable (Zellers et al., 2008). By means of this function, they can help to consolidate ideas and opinions regarding the research (Cross and Oppenheim, 2006).

Types of abstract

In this chapter, we are going to discuss one of the most important aspects of abstracting, the types of abstract.

Theoretically, there are many different types of abstract. In practice, however, there are three:

- the indicative abstract;
- the informative abstract;
- the indicative-informative (mixed) abstract.

While we will discuss these under separate headings, there will be, nonetheless, a constant need to make comparisons between them as their typology builds on both similarities and differences between the different types.

In the introduction in Chapter 1, we have already mentioned practice-oriented online writing guides. When defining our concepts in Chapter 2, we also mentioned them. Let us consider again the guide by Kilborn (1998). This guide enumerates the characteristics of indicative and informative abstracts by pointing out that informative abstracts:

- communicate specific information from the original;
- include the purpose, methods and scope of the original;
- provide the original's results, conclusions and recommendations;
- are short – from a paragraph to a page or two, depending upon the length of the original;
- allow readers to decide whether they want to read a given paper.

On the other hand, indicative abstracts:

- tell readers what information the original contains;
- include the purpose, methods and scope of the report, article or paper;
- do not provide results, conclusions or recommendations;
- are always very short, usually under 100 words.

These points show how many questions affect informative and indicative abstracts. In addition to this, the comparison displays many of the similarities and differences between the two opposing types. A more detailed treatment of these is nevertheless still necessary.

Informative abstracts

Informative abstracts are regarded as more important, more popular and more frequently used than indicative abstracts (Collison, 1971) to the extent that the informative abstract is often identified with 'the abstract' as such, even though we know that all types of abstracts serve useful purposes (Cleveland and Cleveland, 1983).

As regards the nature of informative abstracts, Procter (2008), for example, states that they should represent as much as possible of the quantitative and qualitative information found in the document and also reflect its reasoning. This is one of the most important features that we can use to define the informative abstract. In doing this, abstracts should contain the scope and purpose, the methods employed and the kind of treatment given, the results obtained, the conclusion and the author's interpretation of the results (Collison, 1971).

Informative abstracts have often been compared to a skeleton with the flesh missing. This means that the reader is given enough detail to reconstruct the whole (Cleveland and Cleveland, 1983). This metaphor could seem a little suspicious as it reflects a thinking that is not strictly scientific. Nonetheless, good metaphors can be very useful. The idea of a skeleton links up with the conception of an informative abstract as a miniature version of the original text (Day, 1988; Rathbone, 1972).

While all the above approaches may be regarded as valid, we can get a much more exact picture about informative and indicative abstracts if we examine their linguistic nature, and it is easier to do this if we concentrate for a moment on indicative abstracts. Indicative abstracts always contain some kind of (often implicit) reference to the original (Kuhlen, 1984). This reference can take the form of: *The author* ... or *The article (paper)* ... or *(In) the (abstracted) document* ... In addition, Rowley (1988) points out that indicative abstracts abound in phrases such as *is discussed* and *has been investigated*.

References to the original and to its author(s) are often in an implicit form. That is the reason why the passive voice can be used in indicative abstracts whereas it is advisable to use the active voice whenever possible in informative abstracts (ANSI, 1979).

Fidel (1986) gives an example that illustrates the difference between indicative and informative statements mentioned above. She points out that a sentence such as 'health care facilities in urban areas are more modern, more cost-effective, but less user-oriented than those in rural areas' which might be found in an informative abstract would correspond to 'health care facilities in urban and rural areas are compared' in an indicative abstract.

It is also useful to direct our attention to the markers of cohesion, which can also be found in originals. *This paper aims to* ... or *The results of this study show* ... and the like are important from the viewpoint of organising original texts. They are, however, not needed in abstracts and excluding them saves on the number of words and enables the inclusion of more useful information from the original (Guinn, 1979). This applies to the highly specialised target audience of professionals that values information (Chan and Foo, 2004), of which kind is the audience for abstracts.

Thus indicative statements differentiate indicative abstracts from informative ones. On the other hand, such statements make the writing less economical. Informative statements, in contrast, are statements that can be found in any primary (original) text (Roberts, 1982). Informative abstracts thus concentrate on what the original says and retain in condensed form the inherent thinking of the original (Guinn, 1979).

It is not difficult to see that there is a kind of synthesis here between metaphoric approaches to the nature of informative abstracts and more exact explanations based on the existence of references to the original.

Whichever approach we use, we need to recognise that informative abstracts are formed in a way that differs little from original texts. We can see this especially clearly if we remove such elements as the identification of the source, the (eventual) signature or initials of the abstractor, etc., which clearly show the secondary nature of the abstract. We also need to recognise that informative abstracts are generally longer than indicative ones (Rowley, 1988). Taking this all into consideration we can begin to obtain an overall view of informative abstracts.

Another distinctive feature of informative abstracts is that only they can serve as substitutes for the original. Informative abstracts are designed to provide useful information directly. They are consequently able to make it unnecessary for the user to consult the original for further information (Ashworth, 1973; Cleveland and Cleveland, 1983; Cross and Oppenheim, 2006). Informative abstracts thus have the dual function of aiding the assessment of document relevance and serving as substitutes for the original.

Roundy (1982: 35) explains that informative abstracts can stand alone because they give details about each section of the original and present the main facts of the original, thus allowing the reader to decide whether to continue further with the reading or not if they already know them.

At the end of the day, we have to admit that it is much more difficult to actually produce informative abstracts than it is to understand the conceptual differences between informative and indicative abstracts (Manning, 1990).

Indicative abstracts

According to a commonly shared opinion, indicative abstracts indicate the content of the original in general terms, but do not report the actual content (Rowley, 1988). In other words, indicative abstracts only tell about the original, not what the original contains (Roundy, 1982). This means that indicative abstracts introduce the subject to readers. To find out the author's results, conclusions or recommendations, readers have to consult the original (Kilborn, 1998).

How should these statements be interpreted? Informative abstracts present as much as possible of the qualitative or quantitative information found in the original (Cross and Oppenheim, 2006). Indicative abstracts, on the other hand, resemble tables of contents in narrative style (Cain, 1988; Hughes, 2006; Waters, 1982). This latter metaphor makes the nature of indicative abstracts clearly visible.

Indicative abstracts are often called *descriptive* (Kilborn, 1998). This comes from the fact that, by indicating the content of the primary source, they describe it, while informative abstracts present the information using a kind of prose that could be called narrative and expository. Goldbort (2002: 26) puts this as follows. Indicative abstracts (also called descriptive and sometimes 'topical' abstracts) in effect act as tables of contents for the article put into prose (often paragraphs). They are written about the article, 'rather than transmitting the information contained in it'. They tell readers 'about the kind of information the article contains, focusing on the research problem and providing an abbreviated and indirect description of the methods'. They tell about the paper, and 'rather than encapsulating the actual results and conclusions, [their] sentences convey the different aspects of discussion'.

In consequence, the treatment of information in indicative abstracts is more superficial (Rowley, 1988). Indicative abstracts can be written quickly and economically and require less perception and subject expertise than writing informative abstracts (Rowley, 1988). Ease of use is to be found on the side of both the abstractor and the reader.

If we accept the possibility of some kind of substitution, it should be recognised that indicative abstracts are not intended to act as document substitutes as they are no more than sophisticated selection aids. They only predict the structure of the original, thus cannot stand alone because they have a descriptive rather than a substantive nature (Day, 1989; Roundy, 1982).

However, we should not forget that not being able to stand alone doesn't mean that indicative abstracts are not self-contained, that is understandable without reading (consulting) the primary text. In Chapter 2 on definitions, we have already declared that any kind of abstract is self-contained in this sense. In this context, apparently, standing alone means rather the ability to substitute for reading the original.

Indicative-informative abstracts

It is often necessary to combine the informative and indicative abstracts into a mixed type, the indicative-informative abstract, which is said to be more common than the pure types (Aucamp, 1980). In this regard, Ashworth (1973: 125) is of the following opinion:

It is doubtful, however, whether there is any great value in drawing a rigid distinction between these types of abstract [the indicative and the informative abstract]. Almost always in practice the ideal abstract will combine the characteristics of both types and in any one abstracting publication the amount and kind of information presented will vary with the importance and source of the document under consideration.

While this is true, we should point out that differentiating between indicative and informative abstracts is still important, both for theory and practice, even if it is not easy to see the differences between them (Koltay, 1997b).

Indicative-informative abstracts present a mix: parts of the abstract are written in an informative style, while content of minor significance is treated indicatively. Such abstracts can achieve the maximum information in a minimum length (Rowley, 1988). Indicative-informative abstracts consist of both indicative and informative statements. This means that these abstracts reflect the more important content of the original in a way identical to informative abstracts, while less important content is only indicated using statements that contain some kind of reference to the original.

Different functions

As Collison (1971: 27) points it out, 'Informative and indicative abstracts perform different functions and normally an original that lends itself to one form is not suitable for the other.' Informative abstracts are most frequently used for articles in science, technology and medicine. These papers usually describe experimental work and discuss single themes. They are not suitable for review articles, for which indicative abstracts are most appropriate (Aucamp, 1980; Cain, 1988; Cleveland and Cleveland, 1983; Lancaster, 1991; Rowley, 1988). By their very nature, review articles are already secondary thus their structure differs from the other article types (Montesi and Urdiciain, 2005a). Most of them are lengthy texts from the social sciences and humanities and often contain a high number of individual and disjointed ideas (Aucamp, 1980: Lancaster, 1991; Rowley, 1988).

Indicative abstracts can provide the best starting point for users who know what the themes should be but are unclear of the rhemes as they look for documents in unfamiliar fields of knowledge. By contrast, informative abstracts are appropriate for researchers who look for documents that treat subjects at the forefront of research and which will be mentioned in the rhemes of texts (Hutchins, 1993). We need to explain this further. One of the generally accepted dichotomies in linguistics is that of the *theme* and the *rheme*. The theme represents elements which are related in some way to the preceding text, elements that have been mentioned prior to a particular point in the text. They are recoverable from the text itself or from the extra-linguistic situation. (Extra-linguistic knowledge is based mainly on our knowledge of the world.) The rheme expresses information which is in some sense new to the reader. It contains those elements that have not been mentioned prior to that point in the text and are not recoverable from the extra-linguistic context. We can also say that the theme states what the writer is going to talk about in that sentence while the rheme expresses what they intend to say about it (Hutchins, 1977; Nwogu, 1995).

One source – different abstracts

Abstracts are domain-dependent in the sense that their sources are domain-dependent themselves, that is they reflect scholarly content of different disciplines. On the other hand, abstracts are also goal-dependent (Pinto, 2003b), which is the reason why many different abstracts can be derived from one original (Rowley, 1988). We can even say that there are potentially as many abstracts as there are different user needs: reflecting any of them will result in a new abstract (Pinto, 2003b).

Type and function

As explained in the previous subsections, there is a close connection between the types of abstract and their functions. This connection is the most pronounced in the case of substitution. Only informative abstracts can act as substitutes, provided that superficial or outline knowledge of the documents' content is satisfactory. Indicative abstracts cannot fulfil this function (Houp and Pearsall, 1988; Rowley, 1988).

The objectivity of the abstract

'Stick to facts. Drop sentiments.' This rule presented by Endres-Niggemeyer (1990: 14) very much expresses the foundations of objectivity in abstracting. While the rule is valid, the situation is much more complicated.

Abstracts claim documentational objectivity. In general, this means that the abstractor should be as invisible as possible (Kuhlen, 1984). The word *documentational* acquires here especial importance. It means that this is a limited objectivity because it is based on personal decisions, that is abstractors have to make decisions about the importance of information found in the original. For these decisions they use their personal knowledge base and in doing so subjectivity is introduced into the system to an extent (Nohr, 1999). We will discuss this in more detail in Chapter 4 which addresses issues related to the abstractor.

Documentational objectivity itself has two different levels: it can be absolute or relative. Absolute documentational objectivity means that the abstract contains only information that appears in the original. It should add no new information but simply summarise the original content (Kilborn, 1998). Nor should abstracts disagree with the text of the article (International Committee of Medical Journal Editors, 1982). The requirement to observe absolute documentational objectivity is in many cases left out of consideration, especially in author abstracts, even if the 1997 ANSI standard expressly forbids the inclusion of information or claims not contained in the document itself (ANSI, 1997).

The level of objectivity in originals themselves can vary significantly. The quantity of information contained in scholarly papers may be lower than the information actually produced during scientific research. Content can also be distorted to a certain extent, caused by the tendency not to represent all the ideas, data, results, etc. in scientific documents. In addition, articles show the research process as 'simple, precise, profitable and the conclusions derived – inevitable' (Trawinski, 1989: 694). This is the reason why we do not usually find false starts, mistakes or difficulties with the research process reflected in the literature.

Nor must we forget about the existence of different points of view. Since every author has a specific point of view, authors always have different perspectives and they sometimes leave out relevant information (Paul, 1993). Nonetheless, this does not mean that absolute documentational objectivity does not exist. Objectivity means reflecting the content exclusively to the extent to which it is available in the text of the article. There seems to be agreement on this, while relative objectivity is a more controversial issue and poses the question: should abstracts be critical or not?

Arguments for critical abstracts

Cleveland and Cleveland (1983) state that good abstracts avoid both the bias and personal viewpoints that may be introduced by critical comments. The job of an abstractor is solely to reveal content; abstractors themselves should be invisible in the final product. On the other hand, they add, in-depth analysis and synthesis of information and a more qualitative evaluation require a critical abstract. Maizell et al. (1971) also argue that there is room and need for both critical and non-critical abstracts.

If considered acceptable, what are critical abstracts capable of? They not only describe the content, but also evaluate the work and its presentation. They indicate the following:

- depth and extent of the work;
- the significance of the study;
- the adequacy of the experimentation and survey methodology;
- the assumed background of the intended audience. (Rowley, 1988)

Author abstracts may show subjectivity and persuasion. This is the reason that Pho (2008) challenges the general assumption that abstracts are objective and impersonal. He states that authorial stance does exist in abstracts, although the extent of the author's involvement may vary. Stotesbury (2003) also points out that persuasion in abstracts is expressed both implicitly and explicitly by different linguistic means.

Pho (2008) found that the use of sentences like '... plays an important role in ...' serve as a kind of promotion, an observation with which we concur. Clearly, this does not negate our argument above concerning the problems related to critical abstracts. In the concrete case, for example, the claim for importance presumably comes from the original and consequently does not contradict the requirement for objectivity. We must not forget either that these studies may indicate instances that could simply be deviations from the desirable, because author abstracts may show deficiencies that we will address in a subsection below.

Arguments against critical abstracts

At the end of the previous subsection we suggested that there may be a case against subjectivity and criticism in abstracts. There are certainly many who argue that abstractors are obliged to avoid comments of their own (Cleveland and Cleveland, 1983). As noted by Slade (1997), abstracts are designed to describe documents, not to evaluate or defend them. Collison (1971) adds that abstracts lose much of their value by being critical. The 1979 ANSI standard simply states that critical abstracts are an uncommon form as they contain evaluative comments on the significance of the material abstracted or the style of its presentation (ANSI, 1997).

Many abstracting services do not permit abstracts that represent a critical approach. Maizell et al. (1971) provide a number of possible reasons for this. For example, there may not be many abstractors who are able and willing to write critical abstracts, which take more time to write, are longer and reach their audience late.

There is another possible reason for this: the existence of quality control in journal publishing. Most papers have gone through an editorial review process before publication and are thus regarded as reliable. In addition to this, readers prefer to make their own judgments about the quality of an article. In any event, the viewpoint of the abstractor is not necessarily any more valid than that of the author. They also add that:

> In a critical abstract the abstractor not only describes the content of the document, but also evaluates the work and the way it is presented. This kind of abstract can save time by pinpointing documents of special significance and value. The purpose of the critical review is not to duplicate the refereeing process but to provide an appraisal of the relationship of the selected article to the rest of the literature and evaluate its worth to the potential reader. (Maizell et al., 1971: 65)

Note that in the last sentence the term 'review' is used instead of 'abstract'.

Another line of argument is based on the assumption that critical abstracts fall within a different genre to that of the abstract: they become reviews (Cleveland and Cleveland, 1983). This would seem to be the case. The review is a genre with an outspoken critical element as it not only briefly describes the content of a text but also expresses the reviewer's opinion (Russel, 1988). The other difference between an abstract and a review is that reviewers not only summarise the contents of the original, but may also devote much of their review 'to a few aspects on which they have specialized knowledge, which is unjustified in the case of abstracting' (Collison, 1971: 26). In this regard, it is advisable not to forget that reviews (in this sense) are written on books, while the source of any abstract is an article.

A different and much stronger line of argument raises ethical concerns and emphasises objectivity in terms of questioning the usefulness of critical abstracts. This issue is undoubtedly related to abstracts prepared by someone who is not the original author. Notwithstanding this, the issues related to criticism are complex. Exercising criticism on the work of other researchers is a natural and important element of scientific research and publication. It is obligatory for any scholarly article to have a literature review that draws a picture about research published before the work being reported on. This is the starting point of every article. When doing a literature review, it is advisable to include not only literature that supports the argumentation of the given research, but also articles that contradict it. This requires a critical analysis of such articles. Critiquing the work of others is, anyway, part of the literature review. Otherwise, it would be fairly difficult to find that gap in knowledge or a problem in the field that serves as one of the main justifications of a scientific study. This gap then needs to be filled or the problem has to be solved (Connor and Mauranen, 1999).

Criticism on someone's work can be made public in the form of published 'Letters to the Editor'. In principle researchers can freely submit such letters in order to let other scientists know their opinion about a specific topic and encourage the entire community to witness and even take part in a public debate. There are, apparently, no officially stated acceptance criteria for letters to the editor and editorial boards will decide whether and when they publish them (Magnet and Carnet, 2006). Thus the critique expressed in letters to the editor can be answered and refuted by the author whose work has been criticised.

In abstracting journals and databases there is no place for and in principle no possibility for publishing any reaction to criticism. The authors concerned cannot respond to the critical remarks. Researchers thus cannot react to critique expressed in abstracts. The rather obvious conclusion is that the only acceptable way to express criticism is not to write an abstract on a given article (Rowley, 1988). As my personal abstracting experience shows, this happens from time to time. This is summed up by Ashworth (1973: 134) in the following way:

> While attention may be drawn to an obvious error, giving little space to the abstract or ignoring the article entirely is the only acceptable way of showing lack of value. As space cannot be allowed in the abstracting journal for authors to reply it is at least unfair to adopt a critical style.

This is the reason that critical abstracts are rare and why most abstracting services rely upon the refereeing procedure to eliminate insignificant and inaccurate documents (Rowley, 1988).

The case of Mathematical Reviews

Despite well-founded counter-arguments, examples of critical abstracts may still be found. The question of critical abstracts is thus much more complex and requires more than a yes/no answer. Despite well-founded counter-arguments, examples of critical abstracts may still be found. The real question is: under what circumstances are they used? The following case of *Mathematical Reviews* goes at least some way to answering this question.

First of all, it is necessary to clarify whether *Mathematical Reviews* is an abstracting database or not. According to a *Wikipedia* article, it is. Nevertheless, the same article goes on to say that the reviews in *Mathematical Reviews* often give detailed summaries of the contents (*Mathematical Reviews*, 2008). This contradiction is nothing more than an example of ambiguous terminology and inconsistent use of terms. As we pointed out earlier, this is an unfortunate peculiarity of abstracting.

No doubt, critical abstracts do exist in *Mathematical Reviews*. The Guide for Reviewers (2008) for the database indicates that reviews may include a positive or negative evaluation of the item. It goes on to say the following:

> Negative critical remarks should be objective, precise, documented and expressed in good taste. Vague criticism offends authors and fails to enlighten the reader. If you conclude that the item duplicates earlier work, you must cite specific references. If you think that the item is in error, the errors should be described precisely.

The authors of the Guide also remind reviewers to take into account the fact that the database does not include author responses to critical reviews.

It is not easy to document, but seems to be true that the possibility of critique in the abstracts of *Mathematical Reviews* helps abstractors obtain a certain professional prestige. This prestige is higher than that which can usually be achieved by writing abstracts. Writing abstracts for abstracting services is a useful activity. It can eventually bring some financial benefit to the abstractor, but its main value lies in informing fellow researchers and colleagues in the profession about new developments, as well as serving as a means of professional development for the abstractors themselves. No matter how and why they are useful, abstracts are not regarded as scientific publications. The number of abstracts written by a researcher does not count, for example, towards promotion or in the evaluation of research, as monographs, conference papers and articles, etc. do. The case of *Mathematical Reviews* seems to be different.

Abstracting there is regarded as a scientific activity, most probably because of the critical character of the abstracts.

Once more on objectivity

In summarising what we have said about critical abstracts, we want to remind abstractors to beware of a natural tendency to confuse their own interests and lines of thought with those of the author of the original (Collison, 1971).

When we select articles to be abstracted, as well as when we indicate what type of treatment they deserve, evaluation is taking place. However, this is not the same as being critical. Opinions differ, but for most purposes, the abstractor's standpoint has to be objective and impersonal, with no attempt at individual interpretation or polemics (Ashworth, 1973). Objectivity comes across in the style of the abstract as well. For example, the abstract should not include emotional or expressive elements of style that could give it an individualistic tone (Gläser, 1990).

A more theoretical approach to the issue of objectivity is as follows. In the process of abstracting, the influence of the recipient (addressee) on the primary text is weakened. In other words, the process of abstracting is characterised by a neutralisation of the recipient of the message. In metaphoric terms, we can also say that the recipient is confined to the boundaries of the abstract and the message addressed to this recipient remains enclosed in the text. It can be also said that abstracting communication occurs not between subject and recipient, but is transformed into a relationship between subject and object (that is abstractor and primary text). The representation of the context will be determined by the primary text itself and not by its recipient.

Abstracting is an example of communication where the individual does not need to appear as a carrier of personal values, views and opinions. Individuals in abstracting are anonymous communicators. We can even say that they have no right to display their views and opinions, even if those differ from the ones fixed in the primary text. This situation underlines the role of the individual as a tool (Radzievskaya, 1986).

At the bottom line, we tend to agree with the view that does not favour critical abstracts, as succinctly expressed by Cleveland and Cleveland (1983: 164): 'It is difficult enough to avoid bias, why deliberately introduce it?'

The author abstract

As defined earlier, the author abstract is an abstract produced by the author of the original. Our above discussion has already demonstrated that despite much similarity with abstracts written by someone who is not the author of the original, author abstracts have their own characteristics and problems.

The importance of author abstracts

The nature of author abstracts in scientific journals has been changing over the years with the changing physical format of the article. These changes have facilitated searching and reading.

The author abstract is an author's best opportunity to awaken the interest of the reader. It is one of the most important parts of the article as it is often the only part of it that is read (De Guire, 2006; Pinto, 2006).

Though the numbers are not meant to be significant, Montesi and Urdiciain (2005b) found that out of six bibliographic databases covering two areas (education for the humanities and agriculture), only two employed abstractors; the others used author abstracts when they were available. In addition to this, we know that 91 per cent of 3,741 journal titles available in the *Academic Search Premier* database contain author abstracts (EBSCO, 2008).

Besides readers of journals, it is not only indexing and abstracting services that rely heavily on author abstracts, but specialised search engines (like Google Scholar) do so as well. The reason for this is that author abstracts are available immediately and are of low cost (Montesi and Urdiciain, 2005a).

Problems with author abstracts

As said above, the use of author abstracts raises a number of problematic issues. Collison states simply that a number of authors are incapable of writing adequate abstracts of their own work (Collison, 1971).

However, what are the concrete issues? Many share the opinion that author abstracts are often poorly written and include an inappropriate quantity and quality of data (Maizell et al., 1971). In this regard, a relatively common failure of authors is to include in their abstracts data and arguments which do not appear in the articles themselves, breaking in this way one of the most widely accepted abstracting rules. As said earlier, abstracts have to be objective, at least in the documentational meaning of the word. Abstracts are intended to convey the original message but nothing else (Collison, 1971). This requirement of absolute documentational objectivity has never been questioned.

It is most probable that inconsistencies between author abstracts and the bodies of articles can be traced back to neglecting the above rule. Pitkin and Branagan (1998), for example, found inconsistencies between data in author abstracts and the article text in medical journals. Data and other information were often reported solely in the abstracts. In their next study of the author abstracts published in six prominent and highly regarded general medical journals, they found a high frequency of such inconsistencies (Pitkin et al., 1999). Data found by Siebers (2001) corroborate this and is confirmed by my own personal experience.

A different deficiency was found by Busch-Lauer (1995), who studied German medical author abstracts and their English equivalents. She found that structural inadequacies were already present in the German abstracts. The abstracts studied were characterised by putting emphasis on background information while largely omitting structural parts that are regarded as essential in abstracts, like purpose and scope as well as conclusions.

A further problematic issue is that author abstracts may only reflect what the author considers important and omit material of possible interest to others (Cleveland and Cleveland, 1983; Maizell et al., 1971). On a more general level, this shows a tendency towards being biased and heavily rhetorical to attract the interest of the reader (Montesi and Urdiciain, 2005a). This may have its root in the fact that presenting the results of finished investigations is preferred in journal articles themselves and that not everything is presented in them. False starts, mistakes, complications and the like are not included (Trawinski, 1989).

Authors sometimes use the abstracts simply to promote their papers. This can create misleading abstracts which are unfair to the reader (Cleveland and Cleveland, 1983). Abstracts are not advertisements and we have to disapprove of writing strategies where information is omitted to entice the reader to read the original (Turner, 2003), irrespective of whether such manipulations are fully or partially conscious or not. It is better to recognise that abstracting provides access points to document retrieval rather than constituting frosting on the cake or opportunities for self-promotion or cleverness (Curtis and Bernhardt, 1992).

A number of problems are rooted in the fact that authors are often too close to their papers to be able to give them an objective treatment. This is one reason why they may find it difficult to be impersonal and comprehensive (Cleveland and Cleveland, 1983).

Most authors do not take into consideration that author abstracts will be eventually used for abstracting services. This could be part of the reason why author abstracts do not reflect the point of view of abstracting services (Mathis and Rush, 1975) and represent the needs of the professional community. One might think that mentioning abstracting services here is irrelevant. Author abstracts appear in journals, together with the articles, in which abstracting services do not play any role. There are, however, two points that show the relevance of this thinking. First of all, author abstracts are frequently used by abstracting services thus they are separated from the articles themselves, as we have already mentioned. The second point would seem to be more important. The requirements we set out above ideally are identical to the needs of the readership of scholarly journals, irrespective of whether we are talking about abstracts written by information professionals or author abstracts. Nonetheless, the difficulties that a professional abstractor may find when writing abstracts will, on the whole, be different from those of an author. In addition to this, both the author and the abstractor will perceive user needs differently (Montesi and Urdiciain, 2005b). Moreover, some authors may not fully appreciate the value of abstracts (Maizell et al., 1971).

However, the major cause of deficiencies is likely to be that very few authors are trained, experienced abstractors and usually lack knowledge of the principles, techniques and rules of abstracting (Aucamp, 1980; Mathis and Rush, 1975; Pinto et al., 2008b). There is also a lack of sufficient experience in writing abstracts (Montesi and Urdiciain, 2005a). This would seem to be the reason why 'abstract writers sometimes forget to discuss the relevance of their particular results to the greater field of research' (Turner, 2003).

At bottom, a lack of linguistic (language) competencies among authors may also cause problems. The general skills needed to be able to produce good, clear writing can also be missing, despite the fact that they are especially important when writing abstracts (Staiger, 1965).

All this means that authors need training in abstracting. The related competencies are discussed in Chapter 4 that addresses issues pertaining to the knowledge base of the abstractor. We also argue in Chapter 4 that the writer of the abstract must be someone who is familiar with the subject; in other words, abstracts have to be written by professionals. In principle nobody has more command of the substance of the original than its author (Montesi and Urdiciain, 2005a). The professionals who are required to write abstracts to their articles thus would seem to be the best persons to write them. Moreover, there is practically no one else to do it.

We can also ask the question whether author abstracts are informative or not. Hutchins (1993) is of the opinion that, in general, author abstracts are invariably informative. Experience shows, nonetheless, a great variety in the existence and extent of informative author abstracts. Besides the problems mentioned above, journal editors sometimes do not require abstracts to be informative or do not give attention to the fact that author abstracts become indicative.

On the whole, the existence of defective author abstracts is troubling, because deficiencies and inconsistencies may be reported and disseminated in other works, most of the time without the original context (Winker, 1999).

Advice to writers of author abstracts

Learning to write a good abstract may be just as important as learning to write a good article, because the abstract's quality may determine which and how many users ever see the original document (Staiger, 1965). This is the reason that we have already argued for giving more attention to the fact that abstracting has to be learnt and that the knowledge and skills needed for abstracting can be acquired . This is equally valid in the context of author abstracts. Authors who write scholarly articles should have some kind of training in abstracting or – at least – an awareness of the problems and (perhaps) skills for self-training. One practical aspect of this learning process is that you are instructed to write your abstract when the whole article is finished.

In addition to mentioning the lack of training of authors, Staiger (1965) points out that the first reason for authors being rated as poor abstractors is that they have not much to say. Respected and knowledgeable persons will often write without thinking through what they want to say and who their audience is. No doubt this problem of lack of content exists but a solution is clearly beyond the scope of this book. When preparing an author abstract, authors have to work on their own using the resources of their profession. (The little help that we can offer on this issue may be found in the subsection on abstracting as a professional summarising activity in Chapter 4.)

If you know what you want to say but do not know how to say it, there is no cause for alarm – proper training and reading this book can help you to overcome most barriers.

Preparing author abstracts in a foreign language

One interesting aspect of writing author abstracts is preparing them in a foreign language. In most cases, this language is English. Regarding non-native English speakers Lorés (2004) says that for a long time it had been assumed that writing an abstract was a relatively easy task compared to completing the article itself. She adds that this is not necessarily so, as the abstract constitutes a genre of writing in its own right. Insufficient awareness of cultural, intercultural and cross-linguistic differences and insufficient knowledge of the discursive, rhetorical macrostructure of abstracts in one's native tongue and consequently in a second language can undoubtedly cause problems (Busch-Lauer, 1995).

Hartley et al. (2007) found that providing abstracts in a second language is difficult for many writers. There are a number of possible strategies for authors to cope with the difficulties:

- Attempt the translation by themselves.
- Try automatic translation tools and then improve the texts provided by the automatic translation.
- Ask bilingual colleagues who specialise in the second language to help.
- Ask bilingual colleagues familiar with the discipline and better speakers of the second language to translate the abstracts.

- Ask native speakers of the second language (whether experts in the discipline or not) to rewrite their translation in the second language.

Their advice is not to rely entirely on automatic translation, but to obtain either the services of a native speaker or of a bilingual one. To obtain the services of a bilingual editor who is both familiar with the discipline and the journal to which the paper is to be submitted would seem to be the best solution. Editors and referees of the given journal, in any case, are usually willing to help as well.

Structured abstracts

Structured abstracts may be defined as abstracts that are arranged according to prescribed headings (ANSI, 1997). They clearly appear to solve at least part of the deficiencies of author abstracts pointed out above. Structured abstracts are more common in articles which describe experimental research, although they can also be used for review articles (Hartley, 2004).

First introduced in the mid-1980s, structured abstracts were designed first of all to make the author abstract easier to write. A pioneering organisation in requiring structured abstracts from authors was the Ad Hoc Working Group for Critical Appraisal of the Medical Literature (1987), an international medical journals committee. They proposed at first a seven-heading format for informative abstracts in clinical articles, a proposal which was revised in 1990 in a study by Haynes et al. (1990) who voted for continuing to require authors to submit their abstracts in structured form. The content requirements were, nonetheless, modified to an eight-heading format (objective, design, setting, patients, intervention, main outcome measures, results and conclusion for original articles).

Structured abstracts appear in the 'Uniform Requirements for Journals Submitted to Biomedical Journals' adopted by the International Committee of Medical Journal Editors (1982; revised in 2008). The format required for structured abstracts, nevertheless, differs from journal to journal.

The use of structured abstracts increased during the mid-1990s and spread to other scientific areas. In fields other than medicine, structured abstracts typically contain subheadings and subsections – such as *background, aim(s), method(s), results, discussion* and/or *conclusions* – clarified by the typographic layout.

Nonetheless, the acceptance and use of structured abstracts continues to be controversial. Nakayama et al. (2005) analysed 30 journals in general and internal medicine. They also examined instructions to authors for writing author abstracts. The results show that 61.8 per cent of the articles had structured abstracts and 33.5 per cent used the eight-heading format. Twenty-one journals required structured abstracts in their instructions to authors, eight journals requested the eight-heading format and one journal requested it only for intervention studies.

Structured abstracts, even if not required by a given journal, may be helpful in writing (traditional) author abstracts as they stipulate the structural elements which should be included in the text of the abstract, thus allowing easier identification of the important content. The main phases and techniques of writing a structured abstract are clearly the same as in the case of a traditional abstract. (See Chapter 5 on the practice of abstracting.)

To illustrate what a structured abstract looks like, Figure 3.1 shows an example taken from *Information Research*, a library and information science electronic journal.

Figure 3.1 A structured abstract from Steinerová and Šušol (2007)

Introduction. The paper is based on the study of library users in Slovakia as part of a larger research project on the use of information.

Method. A large-scale questionnaire survey was conducted in 2002 in 16 academic and research libraries with 793 subjects, especially students and educators.

Analysis. The data were analysed with the use of statistical package SPSS. Gender differences are analysed with regard to ways of information seeking, use of electronic resources and publishing.

Results. Results indicate that men prefer individual information seeking and women apply collaborative information use. By sorting user types it was found that women tended to manifest a pragmatic way of information use (the S type). Men confirmed analytic information processing (the A type). Women declared less experience in the use of electronic resources and publishing. Differences in orientation, collaboration and feelings have been noted.

Conclusion. Gender as a variable can be productive for better understanding of the cognitive and social background of human information processing. Findings can inform the design of services and systems and information literacy policies.

Reproduced with permission.

What does an abstractor have to know?

Who can be an abstractor?

The answer to this question is obvious in the case of author abstracts, as their authors are the same as those of the papers. The situation is slightly more complicated if someone is required to write an abstract on someone else's paper. One of the main questions is, nevertheless, whether the abstractor should be a specialist in the given field or not. According to Mathis and Rush (1975), it is better to teach a specialist to abstract than to teach abstractors a subject speciality. Nonetheless, experience shows that there are a number of other professionals, especially librarians, who are able to produce acceptable abstracts without originally being subject specialists but who have acquired professional knowledge.

Chan and Foo (2004: 115) express this somewhat differently, stating the following:

> In an ideal situation it is desirable for the abstract to be produced by a specialist in the discipline, who is also trained in abstract writing. However, this is very difficult to achieve and it is very expensive. Instead, it is more important for writers to understand the reasons why people use abstracts, and that individual users have different needs.

The lack of common knowledge can cause communication problems between summariser and summary (Endres-Niggemeyer, 1998). Nevertheless, this problem is minimal in the case of professional abstracting (at least in an ideal situation) and is excluded in the case of the writers of author abstracts.

If we consider the characteristics of the activities they are engaged in, there are two types of abstractor:

1. Those who prepare author abstracts of scholarly articles written by themselves. These are the authors of the primary texts.

2. Those who prepare abstracts of scholarly articles that have been written by someone else (the authors of primary texts). These are the professional abstractors.

These two types of abstractor share a number of skills, abilities and attitudes. There are, clearly, differences between them as well. In spite of the differences, we will argue that the writers of author abstracts have to be equipped with all the skills that are necessary to become professional abstractors.

The knowledge base of the abstractor

The essence of the abstractors' competencies is the ability to explain the main points of a document in a concise manner (Pinto, 1995). Uso and Palmer (1998) sum up a substantial part of the abstractors' skills and abilities when they state that abstracting 'implies both the complete comprehension of the text to be abridged and the necessary writing ability to create a new version of the source text.'

Abstracts depend not only on the original documents, but also on the abstractors' knowledge base, and abstracts result from the convergence of these against a background of an objective reality (Pinto et al., 2008a). Below we are going to make an inventory of all the knowledge, skills and abilities as well as competencies that are required. In doing so it will not always be necessary to use all these terms, although the reader is advised not to forget that knowledge, skills and abilities, as well as competencies, have different meanings. The Employment and Training Administration of the United States Department of Labor, for example, defines the first three in the following way:

- Knowledge is a body of information applied directly to the performance of a function.

- Skill is an observable competence to perform a learned psychomotor act.

- Ability is competence to perform an observable behavior or a behavior that results in an observable product. (ETA, 2006)

Competence is the ability to perform a specific task, action or function successfully ('Competence', 2008). Note that the terms *competence* and *competency* are mostly used as synonyms.

The ability to abstract information is a basic competence in today's knowledge society, where there is a need to manage and access information effectively. Yet abstracting is not an easy task. It requires purposeful learning because it is a professional activity. In the wider context, it is related to information literacy, a detailed discussion of which you will find later in this chapter.

Abstractors have two basic types of knowledge:

- extra-linguistic;
- linguistic.

Neither is more important than the other, but we can say that extra-linguistic knowledge seems to have features that are more specific for abstracting. For this reason we will discuss it first.

Extra-linguistic knowledge

Abstracts are verbal texts which consist of signs and units of a given language but also carry extra-linguistic information. An exploration of the complex relationship between linguistic and extra-linguistic knowledge is beyond the scope of this text, so we will restrict our discussion to pointing out that extra-linguistic information can be recovered from the situation or from the text itself, but not from its grammatical forms. Extra-linguistic knowledge is based mainly on our knowledge of the world.

On a general level, abstractors are required to have the following attributes:

- intelligence;
- imagination;
- independence;
- the ability to work in an organised fashion. (Endres-Niggemeyer, 1998)

Humans are knowledge-based summarisers. They use general and domain-specific strategies. They refer to general factual knowledge and to highly specialised knowledge of their domain in order to understand information and judge its relevance (Endres-Niggemeyer, 2000).

To be able to write good abstracts, abstractors have to be equipped with summarising skills and knowledge that includes an explicit methodology for summarising

(Endres-Niggemeyer, 1998). Accordingly, the extra-linguistic knowledge of the abstractor consists of the following:

- commonplace knowledge;
- technical knowledge (professional knowledge of the given field);
- knowledge of the users (recipients) of the given abstract (of the interests and needs of the audience);
- knowledge of the specifications and instructions regulating the abstractor's work.

The professional aspect of abstracting dictates that abstractors should be familiar with the subject field, as they have to be able to appreciate the significance of the original's content (Collison, 1971). The ideal level of professional knowledge seems to be somewhere between passing knowledge and expertise (Kuhlen, 1989). Abstractors who are experts in the given field are likely to produce short and general abstracts which require more knowledge on the part of the reader (Mathis-Rush, 1975).

Professional knowledge includes knowledge on the conditions and circumstances of how the primary document (original source) came into existence. Abstractors have to be familiar with the given problem and the results achieved in the given field. This can be turned into a question that abstractors have to be able to answer: *What is important in the given field?*

With regard to the second set of issues, abstractors have to be aware of the communicative intention of the original author. It is therefore essential to be able to understand what it was that the author regarded as important or noteworthy (Belkin, 1993). The knowledge base of the abstractor should thus be sufficient to answer a second question: *What is important in the given context?* (Pfeiffer-Jäger, 1980).

To be competent in answering the above two questions adequately the following knowledge and skills are required:

- rigour, accuracy, consistency and constancy;
- efficient reading;
- the ability to analyse (classify) and synthesise information in a text;
- the ability to recognise and retrieve appropriate information from a text;
- awareness of the various types of abstracts and their application to different texts and contexts;
- knowledge about how to apply abstracting techniques to different types of documents;
- clarity in setting out arguments;
- the ability to assess abstracts. (Pinto et al., 2008a)

We should also add that in the case of humanities abstractors have to be knowledgeable of the related cultures (Tibbo, 1994b).

Interest in the given topic can also influence the work of the abstractor. As pointed out by Yu (2009), a reader's interest, whether cognitive or personal, in the topics with which the given text is concerned influences the choice of information to be included in a summary. In the case of abstracting, there has to be a basic interest in any topic of the profession. Increasing specialisation, however, may cause the level of knowledge and, in particular, the interest in it to vary from topic to topic, even though – as said above – a broad range of knowledge and interest is more beneficial.

In abstracting, document architectures are an important source of knowledge. Professional summarisers should be familiar with the types of document in their domain as they will be concentrating on the document type and its architecture, i.e. schematic structures, also known as *superstructures* (see Chapter 7), during the whole abstracting process. In addition, abstractors have to be aware of the fact that the structure of the original document determines the structure of the abstract and contains indications as to the content to be abstracted (Endres-Niggemeyer, 1998).

There are also regulations (norms, rules and conventions of the profession) that determine the work of the abstractor, though the knowledge that is encapsulated in these standards is, by its very nature, general. Consequently, it does not comprise every possible issue and cannot always be adapted to the practice of abstracting. The situation with abstracting instructions is similar. They are very much dependent on the organisations that issue them and their quality varies (Endres-Niggemeyer, 1990). In many cases abstractors receive only oral instructions (Fidel, 1986). In addition, the majority of instructions address the abstract as a final product and give little attention to the process of abstracting (Pinto, 1995).

The abstractor's goal is to write abstracts on behalf of the user community. The regulations, accordingly, reflect a societal order to write an abstract and this order implicitly includes the requirement to satisfy certain user needs. Commissioned by an organisation, abstractors engage in a communicative activity that not only satisfies the needs but also influences the views of the target community (Pfeiffer-Jäger, 1980). As Cremmins (1982: 105) states, abstractors 'influence the decision-making processes of indexers, researchers and other writers, and contribute to their effectiveness as a function of the quality of the abstracts that they produce.' An important element of extra-linguistic knowledge is thus an awareness of the mission that abstracts and abstractors fulfil.

Linguistic knowledge

Abstractors 'should be clear and concise writers. [They] should also enjoy the challenge of reducing the original to its essentials. A certain, detective-like skill is needed to find the main points in a wordy, badly written article' (Neufeld and Cornog, 1983: 10). These requirements build a kind of bridge between extra-linguistic and linguistic knowledge, the source of which is the text and which consists mainly of the ability to interpret that text.

To be able to study the structure of the primary source adequately and to apply different methods to transform the original text into an abstract with good results, the abstractor has to know the following:

- the linguistic structure of the primary source;

- the linguistic structure of the secondary source;

- the methods by which the linguistic structure of the primary source is transformed and the abstract is created. (Iatsko, 2001)

This last point clearly requires both linguistic and extra-linguistic knowledge.

Linguistic knowledge consists of different competences which we may also term communicative competences. Most of them are related to abstracting.

Knowing and being able to use a language constitutes *linguistic competence*. Knowing the system of rules that define the use of utterances generated for communicative purposes constitutes *linguistic pragmatic competence* (Bańczerowski, 2000b). The need to have linguistic competence and linguistic pragmatic competence originates in a very practical requirement for abstractors to be fluent both in the source and in the target language (Mathis and Rush, 1975). It is not of course necessary that the source and the abstract be in different languages. It is also obvious that 'the most serious fault is when the source language is not well understood by the abstractor' (Mathis and Rush, 1975: 454). This is true even if we engage in that kind of abstracting which does not involve a second language. However, in the case of the humanities, there are special requirements. Abstractors in this field have to be skilled in various languages, because in addition to English-language sources, information resources for the humanities are often based on foreign-language materials (Tibbo, 1994b).

While we are on the topic of linguistic competence, it is important to stress that efficient reading is especially important. Being able to identify and remember the main ideas in a text is the key to the basics of reading comprehension and the ability to become good readers. While superficial reading of a text can provide clues about its content, to understand it requires greater effort (Pinto et al., 2008a). We will discuss reading in more detail in the relevant subsection of Chapter 5.

Meta-information is the main constituent of *meta-linguistic competence* and *meta-linguistic pragmatic competence*. In the terms of communicative linguistics, meta-informative structures partake in the organisation of linguistic communication in general and in organising the elements and parts of the text in particular (Bańczerowski, 2000a). Such structures, however, can be found in primary (original) texts. Library and information science usually has a different understanding of meta-information which it defines as information about information. In the case of abstracting, this latter meaning has prime importance. In this context, meta-information is understood to be information related to the primary document and expresses the relationship between the primary document and the abstract. Nevertheless, this understanding does not exclude the above-mentioned linguistic function. The difference, obviously, is that these assertions are attained not only within one text, but also between different texts, in other words between the original and the abstract. The abstracting process is very much built on the fact that abstracts can be defined as meta-texts, because the abstracting process results in an individual meta-image that lays the foundation of a representation that can then be developed into an abstract. Meta-images seem to have close connection with mental models, especially those that serve to interpret the facts described in order to facilitate comprehension (Pinto, 2006a).

Cultural competence is the ability to use cultural rules. Culture itself can be interpreted as knowledge of the system of rules necessary for generating cultural products. The ability to use the cultural products which already exist in social interaction is *cultural pragmatic competence* (Bańczerowski, 2000b). The cultural background of abstracting is of extraordinary importance, as decisions about the importance of a given piece of information are deeply influenced by cultural factors in a wide sense, even though it is difficult to capture this influence. However, the question of culture is beyond the scope of this book. What we can say is that one special kind of cultural competence is genre knowledge. In a similar way to general writing tasks, abstracting requires more than just knowledge of the topic about which we are writing. Both general writers and abstractors have to know how to communicate the message to the intended audience in the most appropriate and most effective way, in other words how to communicate strategically within a community of discourse (Andersen, 2006). Information literacy also has its cultural knowledge that enables the writer to recognise and use language appropriate to different social situations (Bawden, 2001).

A synthesis: abstracting competencies

We have discussed above the extra-linguistic and linguistic knowledge needed for abstracting and it would appear that the distinction between the two is mostly artificial. There is consequently a need to address the skills, abilities and knowledge required in a more complex way that reflects their interrelated nature. This subsection thus recapitulates what we have said, albeit from a different point of view.

There are four general classes of abstracting competencies:

- general intellectual skills of reading, writing and thinking;
- meta-cognitive strategies of self-monitoring and steering;
- control activities that drive the lengthy intellectual working process of abstracting;
- genuine abstracting expertise. (Endres-Niggemeyer et al., 1995)

The competencies are connected to five broader areas:

- comprehension;
- analysis;
- synthesis;
- organisation and structuring of the information;
- expression.

These areas take shape in different activities as follows:

- reading and comprehension;
- analysis and interpretation;
- synthesis;
- organisation and representation;
- writing up.

Considering this, we can draw up the following list of competencies (consisting of awareness, skills and knowledge):

- knowledge of the appropriate methods, techniques and strategies to identify and extract relevant information from the text;
- awareness of the various types and functions of abstracts;
- knowledge of the specific terminology found in the text;
- general knowledge of the techniques of analysis and synthesis;
- awareness of standards, instructions and recommendations for abstract writing;
- writing skills;
- evaluation skills. (Pinto et al., 2008a)

Self-regulation

The activities and strategies discussed above may be included under the umbrella of self-regulation. Among the abstracting competencies are control activities that can be broken down into general processes of self-regulation and control of the abstracting process that are often inseparable from each other (Endres-Niggemeyer et al., 1995).

Self-regulation is directed towards cognitive processes within ourselves, utilising skills and strategies with volition, carrying out tasks on purpose and with a specific purpose in mind (Wolf, 2007).

Self-regulation is closely related to and is often used synonymously with meta-cognition. Meta-cognition is thinking about someone's own thinking, in other words it is reflecting on and evaluating one's own thinking processes (Granville and Dison, 2005). The two complementary components of this broader notion are *meta-cognitive knowledge* and *meta-cognitive strategies*.

Meta-cognitive knowledge refers to information that learners acquire about their learning. Meta-cognitive strategies are general skills, through which learners manage, direct, regulate and guide their learning. Meta-cognitive knowledge also plays a role in reading comprehension and writing. It can be deliberately activated when conscious thinking and accuracy are required (Wenden, 1999). The ability to think meta-cognitively is essential for undertaking higher-order tasks (Granville and Dison, 2005) like abstracting.

Self-regulation (meta-cognition) fits well with information literacy (see the relevant subsection). The *Information Literacy Competency Standards for Higher Education*, issued by the Association of College and Research Libraries (2000), directs our attention to a framework for gaining control over how someone interacts with information. This is achieved by sensitising learners to the need to develop a meta-cognitive approach to learning that makes them conscious of the explicit actions required for gathering, analysing and using information.

Professional summarisation

In the subsection entitled 'Abstracts vs. summaries' we explained that abstracts come into being in the process of summarisation and that summarisation (summarising) is a much broader concept than abstracting.

In Chapter 2 on definitions, we stated that abstracts are derived texts. An essential characteristic of derived texts is that they select, evaluate, order and condense items of information according to their relevance for a particular subject or purpose (Gläser, 1993).

Consequently, most derived texts come into being in the process of extraction and summarisation of information, analysis and synthesis, all of which play an important role in many forms and phases of general verbal communication (Hutchins, 1987; Eisenberg, 2007; Loo and Chung, 2006).

Summarisation is a higher-level, intelligence skill that goes beyond elementary cognitive activities. It results in summaries, a broad category that covers a number of text types and genres, including abstracts. Different summaries are closely related to each other by the fact that the information source determines what is discussed in them. The source of summaries can be either oral or written discourse. Summaries themselves can also be oral or written (Gläser, 1993).

Seen from a broader perspective, we can say that some kind of summarisation is performed by all readers every time they read a text. The ability to say what a text is about on a general level is one facet of our ability to understand texts (Hutchins, 1977).

Everyday and semi-professional summarisation

Summarisation can be a non-professional, everyday, occasional activity. It can also take a semi-professional as well as a professional form. These levels are extensively discussed and characterised by Endres-Niggemeyer (1998) whose work we will mainly rely on in the following discussion. All three levels of summarisation – everyday, semi-professional and professional – are closely connected to information literacy. There are, undoubtedly, differences even between summarisers involved at the same level as highly qualified people produce better summaries. The most important task at all levels is the reduction of large units of information so that only the most relevant points are retained.

Everyday summarisation takes place when, for example, we relate at home the gist of a recently seen movie or television programme, when we report what happened in a meeting or when we bring together the important content of course materials in order to understand and memorise it better. Most of this type of summarisation is done to suit the occasion and requires no special effort, no preliminary training and no special skills. In these everyday situations, we retrieve the summary content from our own memories and do not use any external source (Endres-Niggemeyer, 1998). Everyday summarisation skills belong to the communication competence of all language users. The extent and tools of selection and abstraction, however, vary with age (Garner, 1982).

The next level of summarisation is an issue for a more limited – although still wide – circle. Semi-professional summarisation is characteristic of professions that require summarisation activities that are repeated, more regular and less spontaneous than everyday life. However, the production of summaries would appear not to be regarded as a main activity and is not an exclusive occupation.

The rules that regulate this activity are weak. This is the reason we call this category semi-professional summarisation. However, the skills of semi-professional summarisation go beyond the competencies that are required for everyday summarisation. For everyday summarisation, normal comprehension is sufficient. What we understand is appropriate for summarisation, and there are no particular presentation problems. Efficient summarisation is different, as it requires learning (Endres-Niggemeyer 1998). Semi-professional summarisation undoubtedly has to be more efficient than the everyday type.

Semi-professional summarisation is performed, for example, when:

- secretaries record the minutes of meetings;

- journalists report on the findings of enquiries or press conferences;

- judges sum up evidence presented in court;

- researchers present oral summaries for fellow colleagues on recent developments in a given field;

- researchers begin their papers with summaries of the state of knowledge in the given field (that is they do a literature review) (Hutchins, 1987; Endres-Niggemeyer, 1998);

- researchers write conference abstracts;

- students take notes at lectures;

- students present shortened versions of different texts at language examinations;

- executive summaries are produced.

If we take the examples of journalists and researchers, it is advantageous for them to master the most important summarisation techniques yet none of them would regard themselves as summarisation professionals.

Though discussed earlier, conference abstracts deserve to be looked at in further detail. Conference abstracts written by researchers are found relatively often because such secondary documents are required in order for conference papers to be accepted. Thus the writing of conference abstracts can be regarded as a typical semi-professional summarisation activity, on the grounds that this activity recurs with relatively high frequency and has apparently weak rules that may change from conference to conference.

Activities related to teaching and learning foreign languages – although still semi-professional – represent a slightly different level, because they require adherence to more explicit rules, even though these rules seem to be less researched than some other types of summarisation. Notwithstanding this, as Uso and Palmer (1998) point out, this is 'not merely a linguistic activity, but also a communicative and discursive one, in which students apply the knowledge previously acquired.' They also emphasise that 'in the attempt to link reading comprehension and writing fluency, summarisation is also a very motivating teaching task. This type of activity implies the use of diverse cognitive mechanisms.' Perhaps the best-known example of such semi-professional summarisation is when students are requested to present shortened versions of different texts for foreign language examinations. Tasks of this type are now being used in international language tests like the new TOEFL (Test of English as a Foreign Language), widely accepted in the United States (Yu, 2009). Nevertheless, in this instance, we should not forget that producing derived texts is secondary to the acquisition of the targeted foreign language. This type of activity represents only one tool which may be employed to reach the goal. It is consequently still semi-professional, even if it is carried out with the help of a teacher.

Proficiency in summarisation

Summarisation competences can be further developed to professional proficiency. Professional summarisers possess more formulation skills than everyday language users, first of all because they are trained in summarisation techniques. They show a professional level of competence. They also apply more knowledge processing and formulation skills than ordinary participants in communication. This allows them to achieve a better performance, greater competence, higher speed and better quality than non-professionals.

For information professionals summarisation is a core qualification. Many are often involved in abstracting during their professional lives (Endres-Niggemeyer, 1998). The organisers of the Aslib abstracting courses stress the professional aspect of abstracting as follows: 'This course reassures participants that abstracting is a learnable skill which we all practise in our daily lives, and shows how we can use our ordinary reading and writing skills more efficiently to improve our abstracting technique' (Aslib, 2008).

The professional nature of abstracting does not mean that all abstractors work full-time. On the contrary, most have no fixed employment as abstractors but carry out this work in addition to their other professional duties. Their abstracting tasks can be related directly to their workplace duties or they may be employed part-time (additionally) by an abstracting service (agency).

Abstractors approach their job with a target in mind. Their task is to produce abstracts (Endres-Niggemeyer, 2000). This is true for both types of abstractors even though the writers of author abstracts do not have a direct or outside 'employer'. This is the mission we have mentioned before.

Researchers are one of the main target audiences of this book and we have already paid special attention to them. Our aim is to satisfy their needs, especially with regard to those who write author abstracts that accompany journal articles. This is especially important, as we are convinced that the often unsatisfactory quality of author abstracts is caused largely by the lack of attention to their properties. Writing abstracts is regarded (unconsciously) as a semi-professional activity at best, although it should be treated and carried out professionally.

Professional abstracting is also related to two important activities undertaken by information professionals: indexing and classification. (These are discussed in more detail in

Chapter 7.) The analysis of the content of a document is a 'common denominator' between indexing, classification and abstracting, and is probably one of the most important activities carried out by any information professional.

As Hutchins (1977: 17) puts it:

> Finding out what documents are about and summarising their contents are the primary functions of abstractors and indexers of all kinds, whether they work for multinational abstracting services, for national bibliographies, for university or public libraries, for specialised commercial or industrial information services, or for any body providing information about published records.

Although necessary for all three levels of summarisation, discourse comprehension (understanding) becomes especially important in the case of professional summarisation. It would be unimaginable to produce summaries professionally without being able to understand the text and its background properly and precisely. This shows that the techniques used for summarisation are closely related to the cognitive processes of text comprehension. The relationship among our concepts here is complex. Summarisation is a tool to represent content. At the same time, it is a tool of comprehension. The reason for this is that one of the constraints of comprehension is the limited capacity of our working memory. To enable comprehension, we store shortened representations in our memory (Endres-Niggemeyer, 1998; Pinto, 2006a).

More information and a more detailed discussion of the above issues can be found in the subsection entitled 'Reading: types and techniques' in Chapter 5, as well as in the subsection 'Abstracting and comprehension' in Chapter 7.

The information to be summarised may either be available as a representation in the summariser's memory or come from external sources such as documents (Endres-Niggemeyer, 1998). In the case of abstracting the source representation is external, as it is concerned with written text on both the input and the output sides.

The activities of non-professional and professional summarisers are fundamentally the same. Both reduce large units of information so that only the most relevant points are retained. However, professional summarisers can summarise the same information with greater competence, speed and quality than non-professionals. They are trained, thus they have a command of a number of efficient summarisation techniques and they have acquired explicit methodologies. This allows them to achieve better performances compared to the summaries produced by those who only occasionally summarise texts. Although the users of summaries produced in everyday, semi-professional or professional summarisation are not passive consumers of information, when our aim is to write professional summaries, summarisation grows more sophisticated.

Professional abstractors are people who have a mission. Their goal is – as already mentioned several times – to write abstracts on behalf of a user community and are commissioned by a particular organisation (usually an abstracting service). Practically no one writes abstracts on their own initiative or for the sake of their own entertainment or education. All this imposes a professional role on abstractors for whom efficiency and technical support are major issues both generally in terms of their profession and in particular with regard to their relationship to abstracting (Endres-Niggemeyer, 1998). Abstractors are directed by their mission, thus they comprehend the text exclusively for the purpose of abstracting (Farrow, 1991).

This seems to be the case only for professionals who write abstracts on papers written by someone else, while the process of writing author abstracts is prompted by an awareness of this mission to a lesser extent. This is not to say that the authors of papers do not feel the proper motivation, but this motivation is only part of their broader desire to have their papers published.

Unfortunately, the fact that abstracting requires professional knowledge is far from being recognised as obvious for and accepted by various researchers and many information professionals. It is often supposed that becoming a university graduate equates to being information literate and therefore capable of writing a good abstract in one's own field of expertise. This comes about despite the fact that the ability to prepare abstracts does not come naturally from existing language instruction, and codified public knowledge about abstracting is meagre (Waters, 1982; Endres-Niggemeyer, 1990). On the whole, abstracting is not a simple task that anyone can do without previous education, as abstracting requires knowledge of certain specific techniques and methodology as well as a great deal of practice (Pinto et al., 2008b).

The information literacy context

When we write abstracts, we have to concentrate on deciding what is important in a text. The skills and abilities related to this are becoming more and more essential in all aspects of life. One of the main constituents of information literacy (IL) is this attention to the importance of information. Information literacy has acquired especial weight in education, and in particular in higher education. Throughout their academic lives most students 'have to condense information from lectures, journals, textbooks, as well as bibliographical sources in order to fulfil certain assignments in their own field of study.' This means that they must be able to recognise the overall structure of a text and distinguish the major issues from the minor (Uso and Palmer, 1998). This quality is a main constituent of abstracting and it shows its close connection to information literacy.

What is information literacy?

The existence of the concept of information literacy can be traced back to the 1970s (Roes, 2001). It is rooted in library user education. Nowadays, evidently, IL has significance within education in a wider sense. It is especially closely related to problem-based and lifelong learning.

The rapid development of digital technologies has resulted in a proliferation of information sources and caused information overload. This development serves as the basis for the information society and the knowledge economy. Both require competent information customers and an informed workforce. Information literacy has developed to meet these challenges and requirements (Andretta, 2005).

There are a number of definitions and descriptions of information literacy. They can be broken down into three types, which concentrate on the following aspects:

1. the use of information and communication technologies (ICT) to retrieve and disseminate information;

2. the competences to find and use information in information (re)sources;

3. the process of recognising an information need and then finding, evaluating and using information.

The third type presents the most comprehensive and most relevant option, as it includes both the use of ICT and the concept of information (re)sources and an information-seeking component which comprises identifying, locating and evaluating information (Boekhorst, 2003).

The well-known and widely used definition of IL by the American Library Association reinforces this, stating:

> To be information literate, a person must be able to recognise when information is needed and have the ability to locate, evaluate, and use effectively the needed information. (ALA, 1998)

People are not born information literate but acquire the necessary competences in the process of socialisation. Information literacy competences are acquired not only in formal education, but also outside the school system in informal ways, both actively and passively (Boekhorst, 2003).

Information literacy has relevance for all ages and is a prerequisite for participating efficiently and effectively in the information society. It is part of a basic human right of access to information (CILIP, 2004). The importance of and background to information literacy are expressed in the following statement from Pinto (2008: 1):

> Mere data accumulation does not drive our society to evolve; the rational, organised, productive and intelligent use of information is an essential factor of progress. The paradigms, models and methods for processing and organising information have undergone significant changes in parallel with the electronic era, placing special emphasis on the development of cognitive, structured, and extremely refined value-added products.

IL and abstracting

Generally, we have to be aware of the fact that knowledge on abstracting pre-dates that on IL. In his book on abstracting, Cremmins (1982), for example, stresses the importance of critical reading without mentioning IL. His arguments, nonetheless, underline the professional nature of abstracting.

Uso and Palmer (1998) speak about abstracting from an ESL viewpoint. What they say, clearly, fits well into the picture of information literacy, even though they do not use this expression. Their statement can be boiled down to the following: it is useful to teach abstracting because it helps to enhance reading and writing ability and this seems to create a holistic view of language use.

Our earlier argument emphasised the fact that abstracts remain important tools in decisions about relevance. Being information literate supposes an ability to find information and to compare it to the searcher's purpose and interests. In other words, information literacy requires decisions on the relevance of information found in literature searches with reasonable speed and accuracy and in a way that corresponds to the circumstances and requirements of today's information environment (Beeson, 2005). This requires a critical approach to information. Critical thinking as well as critical reading and writing undoubtedly pertain to information literacy, and – as mentioned already – this is one of the points where abstracting and IL share an interest. Information literacy itself would not be imaginable without critical thinking skills, which in turn are not possible without critical reading and critical writing skills. The most important critical aspect of abstracting is that we make decisions about the importance of words, phrases, sentences and thoughts. In this regard abstracting is a special case of eliminating details from a complex perceptual field to reveal underlying structures (Root-Bernstein, 1991).

Nevertheless, the critical component of IL is different from critical reading for abstracting. The reason for this can be found in the environment from which the material that is the subject of criticism comes. Papers published on paper or in digital form go through some kind of quality control before being published. These control mechanisms are sometimes very strong as in the form of peer review which allows the strict filtering of manuscripts. Because of this, originals to be abstracted are texts that have gone through a number filtering phases. They have been published in scholarly journals. After that, they have been selected by the abstracting service, by its editor and by the abstractor. This quality makes them different from information sources, the provenance, identity, reliability, genuineness, value and other properties of which are or may be questionable or unclear. It is clear, however, that critical reading for abstracting is still necessary.

Critical reading includes – among other processes – the following:

- determining the purpose of the text and assessing how the central claims are developed;
- making judgements about the intended audience of the text;
- analysing the structure and logic of supporting arguments or methods;
- distinguishing the different kinds of reasoning in the text;
- examining the evidence and sources of the writing;
- assessing point of view, bias and prejudice;
- recognising deception and manipulation;
- evaluating reliability, validity, accuracy, authority and timeliness. (ACRL, 2000; Jones, 1996; Lynch, 1998)

We can ask accordingly a number of questions:

- What is the author trying to say?
- Why are they saying it?
- Who else is saying similar or different things?
- Why should we believe any of them? (Beeson, 2005)

These criteria, actions and questions pertain both to a broad framework of information literacy in general and to abstracting in particular. In the case of abstracting, many of these questions help to identify important information. Identifying the authority and veracity and uncovering bias and manipulation evidently become secondary.

The information literacy aspect of abstracting is especially stressed by Pinto et al. (2008a), according to whom the information-literate student synthesises the main ideas to construct new concepts in the following ways. The student:

- recognises interrelationships among concepts and combines them into potentially useful primary statements with supporting evidence;
- extends initial synthesis, when possible, at a higher level of abstraction to construct new hypotheses that may require additional information;
- utilises computers and other technologies for studying the interaction of ideas and other phenomena.

They also add that information literate students should have the skill and ability to analyse and synthesise information and thus be capable of abstracting the main ideas from documents by selecting, generalising and integrating relevant information. Having achieved this, they use their own words to construct new knowledge while remaining faithful to the original information.

Abstracting builds on the learning component of IL. The nature of learning is, however, much more intentional than in the case of general IL skills. If we want to acquire abstracting skills, conscious, goal-directed learning is needed. We repeat: abstracting is a professional activity.

As seen from the definitions, information seeking stands at the very heart of IL. Information seeking is often considered trivial and regarded as something that everyone can master without training (Andersen, 2006). IL, on the other hand, may include cultural knowledge that enables us to recognise and use language appropriate to different social situations, including thinking and questioning (Bawden, 2001). This is obviously not trivial and it appears in many documents that formulate IL skills. The Association of American Colleges and Universities, for example, requires informed learners to be able to communicate orally, visually, in writing and in a second (foreign) language effectively (AACU, 2002).

Analysing a technical communication course, D'Angelo and Maid (2004) also stress the importance of using information, writing and reading for learning, thinking and communicating. The course goes even further, calling on students for an understanding of the relationships between language, knowledge and power and for a recognition, understanding and analysis of the context within which language, information and knowledge are communicated and presented.

Abstracting is a writing activity. In this respect, it is also closely connected to IL. We know that reading and writing skills themselves are not considered trivial. Writing research, however, focuses on what makes people better at composing and writing texts (Andersen, 2006). Abstracting, in contrast, is a special case of reading and writing. It is based on decisions whether a given content goes into the abstract or does not have a place in it at all. The basis for this is to be able to find what is wanted or needed. Without this basic ability of information literacy other aspects of using or evaluating any information are impossible (Wolf, 2007).

The ability to access information, to be able to find what is wanted or needed, is the cornerstone of information literacy. Without the ability to find information, no other aspect of using or evaluating that information or the products that are produced from it is possible. Learning in general integrates an individual's new and prior knowledge. A higher form of learning is called meaningful learning that especially requires this integration and is favoured by abstracting.

As already pointed out, abstracting involves not only the selection of relevant information but also the identification of the textual structure of the original document (Pinto et al., 2008a).

Abstracting, in the end, fulfils the requirements set by one of the definitions of information literacy:

> Information literacy is the adoption of appropriate information behaviour to obtain, through whatever channel or medium, information well fitted to information needs, together with critical awareness of the importance of wise and ethical use of information in society. (Johnston and Webber, 2003: 326)

It is worth looking at some models of information literacy which may be applicable from the viewpoint of abstracting. The 'Big6' model by Eisenberg (2007), for example, covers tasks beginning with definition and ending with evaluation.

In the fourth stage, which addresses the use of information, we find extracting information. Extraction is preceded by the stage of engaging with information, which means mainly reading. Presenting information is a natural part of the abstracting process and is part of stage 5, synthesis. The model also includes evaluation which is a natural component of a number of different processes, especially writing activities. Two levels of evaluation are proposed in stage 6: judging the product and judging the writing process. Such an evaluation could be integrated into the evaluation of abstracts. (See the relevant subsection in Chapter 5.)

The agenda proposed by Loo and Chung (2006) is closely related to the above model and directs our attention to the important issue of integrating new information with prior information and knowledge. Prior and new knowledge play an important role in general learning. It is easy to see that abstracting favours this integration as it involves not only the selection of relevant information, but also the identification of the textual structure of the original document (Pinto et al., 2008a).

There is also the possibility of aligning the professional requirements put before abstractors with general information literacy competencies by focusing on the third and fifth competencies established in the Information Literacy Competency Standards for Higher Education of the Association of College and Research Libraries (2000). These two competencies are most closely linked to the processes of analysis, synthesis and abstracting of information, both for learning processes and for professional life (Pinto et al., 2008b). Accordingly, people who are skilled in accessing and using information are able to read a text, select the main ideas and extract the information, taking into consideration the purposes and format of the text to be produced.

Those who are equipped with the above competencies are also able to synthesise the main ideas in order to construct new concepts. They recognise the interrelationships between concepts and assemble them in new, potentially useful, primary statements (ACRL, 2000).

It is in LIS education that abstracting receives the most attention. While very few IL competencies are explicitly taught in higher education, indexing and abstracting courses are directly related to core information literacy competencies (Pinto et al., 2008b).

Like information literacy itself, abstracting is closely connected to text comprehension. While it is beyond the scope of this book to discuss these complex questions exhaustively, we will, nevertheless, touch upon some of the issues in the relevant subsections of Chapter 7.

Abstracting education

The goal of abstracting education is to form the knowledge base of those who are involved in abstracting. Such education is also directed towards producing the appropriate skills, abilities and knowledge required to become successful abstractors.

In the introduction we mentioned the abstracting courses provided by Aslib. The course organisers stress that abstracting is a learnable skill. We will look here at the most important elements from this course outline.

The course begins with a practical introduction to the key techniques used in abstracting and is aimed at answering the question: what do we want our abstracts to achieve? The course includes knowledge and skills on what to include in an abstract and writing abstracts that are accurate, comprehensive, stylish and prepared with speed (Aslib, 2008). We will address the majority of these aspects in Chapter 5.

On completing the Aslib course, it is promised that the participants will be able to:

- scan documents rapidly;
- identify the key content of documents;
- summarise that content;
- write to a prescribed length and deadline.

One of the exercises is writing a postcard (Aslib, 2008). The skills of sending written messages using limited space pertain to everyday summarisation that we mentioned earlier and represent a good preparatory exercise to abstracting.

My personal experiences in teaching abstracting come from the period 1992–2002. During that time I was a part-time faculty member in the English translation programme at the Technical University of Budapest (TUB). This programme still exists and contains abstracting as an integral part of a course called Professional Documentation (PD). PD is a course designed to make students of translation acquainted with those written genres of linguistic mediation that are not translation but which a translator may be required to write. One of these – and perhaps the most important – is the abstract.

At TUB the state examination which concludes the education of translators includes abstract writing. During this examination, an abstract of a technical article in a source language (English, German, French, Russian, Spanish and Italian respectively, depending on the given programme) has to be prepared in Hungarian.

This type of abstracting education very much builds on the fact that the students have a good chance of becoming good abstractors. They have the necessary language skills, will be equipped with abstracting skills and present the ideal expertise required for this activity. That is, they have enough understanding of the subject but are not necessarily subject experts in a narrow field. This is a result of their background as they are studying an academic subject or have already graduated and are receiving education in translation that includes abstracting knowledge and skills, imparted in PD. The students thus have both the necessary professional knowledge and language skills (Koltay, 1997a).

In our course, we drew the attention of the students to the necessity of being critical with author abstracts because their quality varies greatly. We made them aware that good author abstracts may be found, but abstractors should not rely on them as the only source of information. This was easy to understand in practice.

Abstracting was preceded by the analysis of the structure of scholarly papers. As a result, the majority of the students knew that most documents contain background information as well as descriptions of well-known techniques, equipment, processes and results. All we had to add was that these have to be omitted in abstracts.

Students were also made aware that a typical scientific article shows a structure which corresponds to one of the following patterns: Introduction – Methods – Results – Discussion/Conclusions (IMRD/IMRC). We pointed out in addition that this structure is less typical in the field of social sciences and humanities (Koltay, 1997b).

We know that abstracting courses often concentrate on the structure of articles in (natural) sciences, as it is much easier to follow their standardised form. If possible, however, it is beneficial to teach students according to the conventions of abstract writing in their own fields, especially if it pertains to the humanities (Stotesbury, 2003).

In PD, it was easy to become acquainted with the steps which a good abstractor has to take. Comparisons with translation helped a great deal in this.

Practice concentrated on writing informative abstracts. Exercises included looking for topic sentences in texts, analysing text structures and the headings of scientific articles along with other types of texts. Abstract writing was carried out with the teacher's assistance both in small groups and independently, with a subsequent analysis of the work done and discussions of possible alternatives, failures and improvements (Koltay, 1997b).

The experiences acquired since 2004 with Hungarian LIS students differ only in one aspect: foreign languages play a lesser role in their abstracting education. This suggests that besides providing all the necessary theoretical knowledge, also presented in this book, practical advice is of the utmost importance. Consequently, rules play a distinctive role.

In order to produce effective texts, students have to master the textual organisation and other key linguistic features that constitute a successful abstract (Martín Martín, 2003). This is especially important as the problems related to presenting the main ideas that have been selected accurately and thoroughly in coherent sentences is often much more difficult than the selection itself (Pinto et al., 2008b).

In addition, it is not enough to focus solely on the abstract as the final product. If we ignore the stages necessary in the creation of an abstract, we cannot see which competencies and abilities need to be strengthened in order to write a successful abstract (Pinto et al., 2008a).

Last, but not least, we must say a word about topic sentences. I always had a mixed experience with exercises which were aimed at finding topic sentences and using them in the abstract. This experience concurs with the observations of Sherrard (1985), who questions the validity of the rules for the selection of topic sentences in light of the fact that topic sentences and the main idea of a text are often confounded. Her findings also show another erroneous assumption that the main idea is always at the beginning of a paragraph. Both observations seem to be important, because we have to see that writers often begin a paragraph at an inappropriate place or start a new paragraph in order to give the reader's eyes a break in the reading (Thistlethwaite, 1991).

A promising contribution to the education of abstractors has been described by Pinto (2008). The *Cyberabstracts* portal (*http://www.mariapinto.es/ciberabstracts/ingles/intro.htm*) has as its aim the provision of a selection of evaluated electronic bibliographic resources that address abstracting. Though initially conceived as an e-learning resource for LIS students, it can be used by any group interested in abstracting, including abstractors, educators and professionals.

The portal groups resources into the following categories:

- knowledge management;
- theoretical framework;
- information representation;
- natural language processing;
- abstract creation – this is the broadest category, which includes several subcategories such as processes, strategies and techniques of abstracting, models (linguistic, cognitive and statistical), standards and typology of abstracts;
- automatic abstracting;
- modelling scientific documents;
- information retrieval and evaluation;
- other resources.

The rewards of abstracting

As a result of our discussion here it should be evident that abstracting is hard work. As Cremmins (1982: 105) explains, it 'requires mental energy, sustained concentration, and self-discipline.' However, Cremmins also directs our attention towards the positive impacts of abstracting. With each new document, abstractors are given the opportunity to master its content. They may receive recognition for well-written abstracts, have the opportunity to improve their writing skills and language proficiency and contribute to the worldwide dissemination of scientific information (Cremmins, 1982). All this is clearly motivating, and if it has aroused your interest, you can study the abstracting process in further detail in the following chapters.

The practice of abstracting: structure, processes and language

Theory and practice go hand in hand to the point that they are almost inseparable. This means that what follows cannot be considered as purely practical – there is always a theoretical background. Nevertheless, those who are more interested in practical issues will find themselves at home here.

Abstracting is 'a series of small challenges: no two are alike, yet the writing must be consistent, accurate and finished on time'. With these words of Neufeld and Cornog (1983: 10) we begin this chapter that deals with the practice of abstracting.

If we accept that abstracting is both a relatively small task and a challenge, we have to add that it is an ambitious and complex activity, which includes not only the analysis of an original text but a new text (the abstract) also has to be produced. Abstracting is the most difficult of all operations normally applied in a document-processing environment (Pinto and Lancaster, 1999). Analysis and synthesis, though commonly treated as two different techniques, are – if properly understood – simply the two fundamental components of the same process. Each is relative to and dependent on the other. Analysis is the process of breaking a complex topic into smaller parts to gain a better understanding of it ('Analysis', 2009). Synthesis means the combination of separate elements of thought into a whole. In other words, it is the move from simple conceptions to complex ones (Pinto, 2006a).

We find less standardisation within abstracting services than, for example, in library cataloguing. This is mainly due to different working practices. Abstracts and indexes are usually produced by publishers rather than by libraries (Fattahi, 1998). The other reason is the complexity of operations that comprise the abstracting process. There seems to be, nevertheless, at least one standard: good abstracts follow the rules of good writing (Staiger, 1965).

The structure of abstracts

Abstracts have a dual structure that consists of inner and outer elements. We begin our discussion with the inner structure, because its construction raises many more questions than the writing of the outer structure.

The inner structure

The inner structure of the abstract is the main structure which contains all the information of the original that was judged important and thus worthy of being abstracted.

As we have said in Chapter 4, to be able to analyse the content of the original and identify the important information in it requires familiarity with the structure of the original. This structure varies across the different fields of knowledge. Articles in journals of the natural (hard) sciences have the most standardised structure, a succession of structural parts along the lines of the various 'Introduction – Methods – Results – Discussion – Conclusions' schemes, often referred to as the IMRD structure. This form is especially typical in papers that describe experimental research, the logic of which may be said to reflect the general shape of an hourglass – from general information to the specific, then from the specific to the general (Turner, 2003).

The IMRD structure is widely used in the social sciences but is almost non-existent in the humanities. These differences originate in the differences in information needs and in the ways in which these needs are articulated. Abstracting in the humanities, consequently, should not simply replicate the abstracting models established in the sciences, but should produce their own (Tibbo, 1994b). The recommendations of many standards are, consequently, useful for writing abstracts if the original is from the natural sciences and (partially) from the social sciences. They are, however, less helpful for humanities abstracts (Hall, 1986; Tibbo, 1992).

An extensive review of the literature by Ayers (2008) shows that the IMRD structure for abstracts is widely accepted. On the other hand he also found that a number of published abstracts in the journal *Nature* deviate from this model, even in articles reporting on experimental research. This may be a signal of change as there does seem to be a tendency for scientific journal articles to become more news-oriented and an increasing use of promotional strategies may be found in scientific journal articles that have been traditionally considered non-promotional texts. However, it has to be noted that these are author abstracts and we are well aware that author abstracts may be different from abstracts written by professional abstractors. They may even be substandard, as described in Chapter 3.

While focusing on how variations in discipline affect the abstract genre, Posteguillo (1996) did not find consistent use of IMRD structures in computer science abstracts, although he was able to observe that similar structures do exist. Studying abstracts in conservation biology and wildlife behaviour journals, Samraj (2005) found that the 'Methods' section appears less frequently than other structural parts. Lorés (2004) reports on an analysis of abstracts from linguistics journals and also found 'Methods' generally lacking. These abstracts usually begin with a general indication of the research context, then reference may be made to perceived gaps in the knowledge of the study or some counter-claim may be raised. The final sections usually announce the main findings. This abstract structure fulfils the function of the indicative abstract in the sense that it reflects the structure not of the whole article, but of the 'Introduction' section. Pho (2008) studied 30 author abstracts in the fields of applied linguistics and educational technology the results of which showed that there were three obligatory parts:

- presenting the research;
- describing the methodology;
- summarising the results.

Koopman (1997) provides a checklist for abstracts written for student papers on computer architecture. Although this structure is tied to a particular field of knowledge and directed towards students, a closer look will be useful. The proposed structure is the following:

- motivation;
- problem statement;
- approach;
- results;
- conclusion.

The latter two elements usually figure in most abstracts and especially in those whose originals follow the IMRD structure. 'Approach' is fundamentally identical to the 'Methods' section while 'Motivation' seems to display more of a pedagogical nature.

All these models can be approached as sets of questions:

- What was the research about?
- Where, why and how was it conducted?
- What does it mean if we compare it to the current state of knowledge? (Carraway, 2007; Procter, 2008)

We can also ask the following questions:

- Why would another researcher be interested in this research?
- What are the most important aspects of the research?
- What information will the reader have to have in order to understand the most important aspects? (Laflen, 2001)

It is worth noting that, although all the structural parts of the original should be reflected in the abstract, they receive different emphasis, depending on their importance (Procter, 2008). As Saggion (1999) points out, scientific papers reflect the process of scientific discovery and represent a complex record of knowledge that, among other factors, contains:

- references to the author(s) in person (name(s));
- their affiliation;
- the problem under consideration;
- their solution to the problem;
- the solution of others;

- the motivation for the study;
- the importance of the study;
- what the author(s) found;
- what the author(s) think.

In doing research, researchers have objectives, use methods, obtain results and draw conclusions. In writing papers to describe research, authors might discuss background information, review relevant literature and provide details of procedures and methodologies.

Some parts of the articles should not be represented in the abstract, either because they provide no new information or because they would take up too much space. In abstracts, there is no place for the following:

- (historic) background information;
- literature review;
- references to the literature;
- detailed description of methods. (ANSI, 1997; December and Katz, 1991)

These aspects will be covered sufficiently in the original itself (Goldbort, 2002).

We have to pay special attention to the title of the original. In most cases, it is unnecessary and improper to repeat it in the first lines of the abstract. Procter (2008) addresses this issue and couples it with the self-contained nature of abstracts:

> An abstract will nearly always be read along with the title, so do not repeat or rephrase the title. However, it will likely be read without the rest of the document, so make it complete enough to stand on its own.

The outer structure

The outer structure embraces the inner. In addition, it consists of the following elements:

- the title;
- the bibliographic data of the original;
- additional elements.

We have already mentioned some of the problems connected with the title. We may add here that it can be identical to that of the original. If the abstract is in a different language to the original, a translation of the title has to be supplied, either by the abstractor or the abstracting service or both in cooperation. Whatever the distribution of work, there is an important requirement for the abstract's title. If the original title is meaningless or unduly general, it has to be extended or a new, interpretative, explanatory title has to be generated. This applies to inadequate titles that may sound good but are meaningless or simply do not contain enough real information, even in cases where the abstract is written in the same language as the original.

The bibliographic data usually include the title of the periodical (journal), year, volume and issue numbers, as well as page numbers. This can vary, depending on the citation style used by the given service. Some abstracting services, especially those that are run by libraries, do not require abstractors to prepare bibliographic citations. They prefer to do them on their own, following standard procedures and strictly obeying the rules that they have chosen.

Additional elements to the abstract include thesaurus descriptors, keywords, etc. The name or the initials of the abstractor – if indicated – usually figure after the abstract (Aucamp, 1980; Pinto, 1992).

There is no outer structure in the case of an author abstract in the sense that the title is not separated from the original paper's title and they are usually not in a different language, although examples may be found where journals require multilingual author abstracts. It would seem that the abstractor's name and initials are also irrelevant in the case of author abstracts, and a bibliographic description of the original is not needed.

The process made simple

The fact that the basic procedural steps of abstracting are similar for all types of abstracts makes their identification easier (Waters, 1982). The abstracting process thus consists of the following steps:

- First reading.
- Subsequent reading(s).
- Writing the first draft.
- Checking the draft against the original.
- Rewriting the first draft.
- Checking and editing the final abstract.
- Writing the final abstract. (Collison, 1971; Rowley, 1988; Taylor, 1984)

An abstracting formulary

The abstracting process can be expressed in the form of rules as follows:

1. Read the primary document. When doing this, concentrate on the main characteristics of the text and then the identification of relevant information.

2. Try to identify the target audience of the abstract.

3. Look for parts of the text that convey self-sufficient statements, methods, results. Other parts should only be skimmed through. Do not decide on the importance of a given sentence or passage until the whole text has been read (Cremmins, 1982).

4. If you do not find any information that can be regarded as important, the reading process has to be stopped as there will be no abstract generated. If you do find important information, continue to read.

5. Define the type of abstract that you are going to write.

6. Define the expected length of the abstract.

7. Read the text again. This time reading is an active process that serves the understanding of the main content.

8. Fix important information in the form of underlining and eventually take notes.

9. To identify important information and form your abstract more easily and appropriately, you could use the following hints and rules (described by Endres-Niggemeyer, 1998):

   ■ Use concluding summaries, headings, tables, footnotes, found in the original, etc. to identify relevant parts of the text.

   ■ Cited authors are important. This is true even if it is forbidden to include direct citations (references) in the abstract.

   ■ Judge the importance of information using your professional knowledge.

   ■ Be careful to reflect only what is included in the original. Do not mix it up with your own opinion.

- What is mentioned positively may be included in the abstract. All negatives should be excluded from it.
- Omit what the author judges to be least important, what is obvious. Leave out minor or marginal arguments and points, what is not done, described, etc.
- Do not say anything twice. Amalgamate analogous statements instead.
- Do not repeat what is already contained in the definition of a concept.
- Delete modifiers with poor content.
- Stick to facts. Drop sentiments.
- Omit rhetorical embellishments.
- Break clumsy constructions down.
- Use synonymous expressions that are shorter, terser than those found in the original.
- If necessary for clarity use examples.
- For named facts, on the other hand, drop examples, pieces of evidence, references, definitions and (additional) explanations or specifications.
- Use common short characterisations for facts.
- Take the result itself, leave out how it came about.
- Take the class, group or aggregate, not its members.
- Use standard terminology.
- Use standard acronyms. If an acronym is not very common, spell it out at the first use.
- No graphics or tables.
- No references. (Endres-Niggemeyer, 1998)

10. Write your draft abstract!

11. Judge your abstract by the following criteria:

- Is there enough important information included in the abstract?
- Are there unnecessary details included?
- What is the level of abstraction?
- Are there any misunderstandings?
- How well is it formed in the target language? (Koltay, 1999)

12. If necessary, amend your abstract by adding important information that was left out, by eliminating unnecessary information and wordy sentences and by improving cohesion with transitional words and phrases.

13. Check grammar, spelling, punctuation and the accuracy of data. It is advisable to read and correct it in print. (Kilborn, 1989)

14. Write the final abstract.

15. During the whole process, consciously observe and keep control of what you are doing.

What should you leave out and what has to be included?

In the previous subsection, we dealt with the two most important questions related to the main contents of abstracts. Naturally, there is more to say about the following issues:

- How do we eliminate unnecessary details?
- How can we retain enough information?

With regard to the details of abstracting, we have already presented the main rules, although some require further elaboration.

Although we have said above that non-textual material (graphics and tables) should be excluded from abstracts, the 1997 ANSI standard is less prohibitive. It declares that short tables, equations, structural formulas and diagrams can be included but only when 'they are necessary for brevity and clarity and when no acceptable alternative exists' (ANSI, 1997: 5).

References to the literature should also be avoided. Nonetheless, there could be exceptions to this rule. Abstracts may sometimes refer to earlier studies or even mention the names of other researchers if deemed essential. However, this has to be done as concisely as possible (Goldbort, 2002).

Abstracts reflect the research itself and not the act of writing, so it is superfluous to tell the reader how the original is organised. Thus sentences that begin with the following or similar expressions can be omitted without damaging the message:

- *It is suggested that ...*
- *It is believed that ...*
- *It is felt that ...* (Hughes, 2006)

As mentioned in Chapter 3, indicative abstracts contain reference to the original. This means that in informative abstracts sentences like those below should be avoided:

- *This article evaluates ...*
- *This essay examines ...*
- *This study presents ...*
- *This report ...*
- *The author ...*
- *The writer ...* (ANSI, 1997; Hughes, 2006)

Unfamiliar terms, abbreviations or symbols should be avoided or defined when they occur for the first time (Chan and Foo, 2001; Procter, 2008). On the other hand, words or phrases used as descriptors or identifiers and terms that complement any descriptors or identifiers that may be assigned to the document in databases could be included in the abstract.

The considerations above are more concerned with the formal side of abstracting than with the selection of important information. The latter will be partially addressed below, as well as in the section on reading techniques. For those who are interested in more detailed background to this section, the section in Chapter 7 addressing the relationship between abstracting and comprehension will be of interest.

When we consider what information is to be included in the abstract, it is easy to see that selecting, ordering and making decisions about the significance of the collected information are core processes of abstracting. Traditionally new information is regarded as worth being included in abstracts. Abstracting is thus characterised by a preference for new information. While this is understandable and acceptable we can still ask the question, in relationship to what is a piece of information new? Newness may be judged differently by different recipients. For example, it may be new in an absolute sense, compared to the total knowledge of humanity. Alternatively, it may be new in comparison to some defined set of knowledge (Novikov and Nesterova, 1991). In addition to its relative nature, newness is not the absolute determinant of importance (i.e. significant information). Old information is taken into consideration, because an abstractor's professional knowledge consists partially of old information. Obviously, abstractors have to be aware that this information is old and they have to determine if there is a need for further, newer information.

In selecting important information, the original author's headings, titles and summaries are of great help. The original text often contains other signals that show where the author puts emphasis. Such highlighting expressions include, for example, the following:

- *To be brief ...*
- *In short ...*
- *My topic will be ...*
- *Primarily ...*
- *It should be stressed that ...*
- *I repeat ...* (Hutchins, 1987)

Originals also contain words and expressions that mark important information. Such markers are extremely helpful in identifying important information to be abstracted, as they direct our attention to information judged noteworthy by the author of the original. Iatsko (2001) compiled a dictionary of such markers which are grouped into the following categories:

1. Aim of the research
2. Existing methods
3. Evaluation of the existing method
4. New methods
5. Evaluation of the new methods
6. Results.

Accordingly, the dictionary looks as follows:

1. Aims of the research –
   - Expressed by nouns: *aim, purpose, goal, stress, claim, phenomenon.*

- Expressed by verbs: *aim at, be devoted to, treat, deal with, investigate, discuss, report, offer, present, scrutinise, include, be intended as, be organised, be considered, be based on.*
- Expressed by adjectives: *present, this.*

2. Existing methods (devices, approaches, methodologies, techniques, analyses, theories, theses, conceptions, hypotheses) –

   - Expressed by nouns: *literature, sources, author, writer, researcher.*
   - Expressed by verbs: *be assumed, adopt.*
   - Expressed by adjectives: *known, existing, traditional, proposed, previous, former, recent.*

3. Evaluation of existing methods –

   - Expressed by nouns: *misunderstanding, necessity, inability, properties.*
   - Expressed by verbs: *be needed, specify, require, be misunderstood, confront, contradict, miss, misrepresent, fail.*
   - Expressed by adjectives: *problematic, unexpected, ill-formed, untouched, reminiscent of, unanswered.*

4. New methods –

   - Expressed by verbs: *present, be developed, be supplemented by, be extended, be observed, involve, maintain, provide, receive support.*
   - Expressed by nouns: *principles, issue, assumption, evidence.*
   - Expressed by adjectives: *suggested, new, alternative, significant, actual.*

5. Evaluation of new methods –

    ■ Expressed by nouns: *advantage, disadvantage, drawback, objection, insight into, contribution, solution, support.*

    ■ Expressed by verbs: *recognise, state, combine, gain, refine, provide, confirm, account for, allow for, make possible, open a possibility.*

    ■ Expressed by adjectives: *new, novel, alternative, significant, actual, valuable, meaningful, superior, fruitful, precise, advantageous, adequate, extensive.*

6. Results –

    ■ Expressed by nouns: *conclusion.*

    ■ Expressed by verbs: *obtain, establish, be shown, come to.*

One paragraph or more paragraphs

Should the abstract be written in only one paragraph or is it allowed to use more? There are rather contradictory answers to this question.

Many sources state that the information should be arranged within the limits of one single paragraph (Collison, 1971; December and Katz, 1991). By examining the guidelines of 11 database producers, Armstrong and Wheatley (1998) found that (where guidance was given) abstractors were always instructed to use only a single paragraph. They add, nonetheless, that conclusions must be drawn very carefully from such a small survey. Ashworth approaches this question more cautiously by saying that in the interests of maximum compactness separate paragraphs are rarely used, while Cremmins (1982) states that abstracting is the organisation of relevant information into a coherent unit which is usually one paragraph long. The 1997 ANSI standard expresses a preference for a single-paragraph abstract, although it adds that structured abstracts consist of several, labelled paragraphs (ANSI, 1997).

On the other hand, we can also find statements in favour of using more paragraphs. Locker (1982), for example, votes for dividing the abstract into several paragraphs. Rathbone (1972) adds that the convention of confining abstracts to one paragraph often leads to extreme overcrowding. In addition, Kilborn (1989) explains that an effective abstract uses one or more well developed paragraphs. She adds that these should be unified, coherent, concise and able to stand alone. Chan and Foo (2001) put this in relatively simple terms. They state that we should write one-paragraph abstracts; for longer originals, however, more than one paragraph is suitable.

This problem related to the number of paragraphs seems to be a question of aesthetic consideration and of habitual practice.

Whether we decide for one paragraph or more, the most important criterion is that a particular physical paragraph has to coincide with the mental one (which has to be an ideal requirement in all writings) and there must be no overlapping of content among the paragraphs (Salager-Meyer, 1991).

The sequence of information

The organisation of the source determines the content of the summary. In the case of well-organised documents, summaries should follow the form of the original. If they are, however, less well organised, it is difficult to produce well-structured summaries (Endres-Niggemeyer, 1998). After all, from the wide range of types of summaries, abstracts pertain to a group that is characterised by the presence of a well-structured source text, the article.

However, in relation to well-organised originals, we have to ask to what extent this happens.

We find the requirement relatively often that the abstract should follow strictly the chronology of the original (Kilborn, 1989). Collison (1971) adds that alterations may misrepresent the original message and make it difficult to identify the parts of the original. In contrast to this, December and Katz (1991) express the opinion that readers do not expect the abstract to repeat the sentence structure of the original. This argument can be substantiated if we regard the identification of the parts of the original as a point of secondary importance.

Another reason for ruling out the need to follow the original author's organisation, proportions and wording is given by Locker (1982). She is of the opinion that the more poorly the original is written, the more changes will be needed in the abstract. On this account, we can also ask the question whether abstracts faithfully portray the form and content found in original texts. The answer is that abstracts do not (always) represent the surface form (the actual words, sentences, etc. we hear or read) of the originals (Lorés, 2004). In Chapter 7, where we discuss the relationship between abstracting and translation, we will provide more arguments for the latter opinion from a slightly different point of view.

The language

Abstracts show a complex linguistic structure. The language used in abstracts is characterised by the use of the past tense and third person and the exclusion of negatives (Ayers, 2008). Let us investigate these characteristics and supplement them with further features.

Complete sentences

The textual nature of the abstract requires that we write in complete sentences that contain transitional words and phrases for coherence (ANSI, 1979, 1997). Such short connecting words do not save much space if left out, but improve readability if used (Ashworth, 1973; Chan and Foo, 2001; Locker, 1982). All this corresponds to the statements about the textual nature of the abstract that we set in Chapter 2.

The past tense

There is a tendency to advocate the past tense: what is described is what happened in the past. Abstracts refer to work done and they are written after the manuscript is finished (Day, 1988; Carraway, 2007). Collison (1971) adds to this that within the abstract, the tense should not be changed, even if we otherwise require the writing style to be elastic.

The third person

The third person is voted for by the American Standard (ANSI, 1979), as well as a number of researchers like Chan and Foo (2001) and Procter (2008). The first person should thus be left out in both the singular and the plural (Hughes, 2006).

Negation and negatives

Negation and negatives can be misleading, as they can introduce concepts, properties, materials, etc. that have not been investigated. If we include them in the abstract, they may produce false hits in information retrieval (Collison, 1971). This is supported by the exclusion of negatives, expressed above as a rule.

Passive or active voice

The use of the passive voice is often proposed, because it helps to neutralise the person of the author and gives emphasis to the information itself (Kilborn, 1989). The ANSI standard points out that the passive voice may be used in indicative abstracts while it is advisable to use the active voice whenever possible in informative abstracts (ANSI, 1979). However, the revised 1997 ANSI standard expresses the preference for using verbs in the active voice whenever possible, but adds that the passive voice may be used for both indicative and informative statements if the receiver of the action needs to be emphasised.

Vocabulary

The vocabulary used in the abstract is also important. The abstractor should use the vocabulary of the author as far as possible, because the abstractor's synonyms could partly confuse the author's real meaning. On the other hand, if the author does not seem to be in control of the language and uses terms unfamiliar to the average reader, the terminology has to be changed (Collison, 1971). As already said before, unfamiliar terms, acronyms and abbreviations should be avoided in general, but if used must be defined the first time they occur in the abstract (ANSI, 1979; Carraway, 2007; Locker, 1982).

It is also important to include in abstracts concepts that characterise the topic of the original and thus help information retrieval tools to find the original document (Fidel, 1986). To foster this, it is advisable to make use of the patterns illustrated by the following example: it is better to write 'middle class and working class' than 'middle and working class' (ANSI, 1997).

Reflections on the abstracting process

The above outline of the abstracting process and its rules will enable you to write an abstract. However, it is advisable to acquire a deeper insight into the process as provided by the following comments.

On the other hand, we have to say that, according to Pinto (2003b), instead of establishing rules for abstracting, abstractors should adopt a strategic mindset which is adaptable to each situation, depending on the relationship between the textual unit, the different contexts and the functions of the source text and of the abstract. She adds that the functions of an abstract depend upon the needs and expectations of the receiver. While this is true, in our opinion there is no contradiction. Being directed by the needs of users and using rules makes the practice of abstracting easier. Needless to say, the rules have to be designed in a way that reflects user needs.

General comments

A more detailed review of the abstracting process requires that we comment on the phases outlined above. The first reading serves orientation and general understanding of the text as a whole. Orientation requires selective reading (scanning) that allows exploration of the text. Readers focus on the basic features of the original in order to acquire a general picture of its content and scope (Palais, 1988). In doing this, abstractors must have sufficient understanding to decide if the items found in the original are relevant or not. Any understanding beyond this point is optional (Endres-Niggemeyer, 2000). This reading phase facilitates not only the search for useful information but is coupled with determining the intended audience and the purpose and type of the abstract (Waters, 1982).

The second and subsequent readings are meant not only to check comprehension, but also to enable an in-depth study of the parts of the text that have been identified in the previous reading phase. Although skilled abstractors who have had long experience may carry out the two phases at the same time (Rowley, 1988), less skilled and novice abstractors should not do so until they feel proficient or until editors and users acknowledge the high quality of their abstracts. The second reading phase also provides an opportunity to mark relevant information. Marking usually takes the form of underlining. There may be a need to make marginal notes which mainly serve to generalise, locate and group specific information. While there is no known scientific inquiry into the role of reading in preparing an author abstract, we may suppose that the reading phases will be different because authors know their own texts in much more detail than abstractors do.

Writing the first draft and checking that draft against the original seem self-evident and require no further comment here.

In the case of abstracts written by abstractors, the entire process looked at above is of course preceded by the selection of the actual original to be abstracted. This selection would be unimaginable without an abstracting service (agency). A representative of the service, usually an editor, selects the papers to be abstracted and suggests to individual abstractors that they produce an abstract. This is the first step in selection. In the second step the abstractors study the proposed texts, then accept or reject them. There is also, however, a third step. After a thorough study of the text the abstractor may still find the text inappropriate for abstracting and therefore deselect it. While this does not happen frequently, in my own abstracting career it has happened a few times.

The helpfulness of guidelines

We know that both abstractors who write abstracts of original papers written by someone else and authors who write their own (author) abstracts can sometimes find helpful guidelines for their task. By studying the guidelines of 123 database producers, Fidel (1986) found that 72 per cent provide their abstractors with written guidelines. An examination of 11 sets of guidelines on abstracting from database producers revealed that there are currently no common standards and very little agreement can be found in the guidelines given to abstractors. In the documents studied guidance varied considerably in length and in content. As a result of this, Armstrong and Wheatley (1998: 369) state the following:

> Guidance usually concentrated on the expected product and they specified the easily measured points, such as the length, broad content, grammar and paragraph structure. When dealing with less concrete concerns, such as the topics represented and specific limitations to be noted, the guidelines tended to be less prescriptive and were more divergent in their instructions.

This supports what was said in Chapter 4 about the limited use of instructions.

Reading: types and techniques

Our reflections on the abstracting process have already dealt with some of the issues that surround reading. However, a more comprehensive review of the role played by reading processes in abstracting seems to be essential at this point.

Though seen from a general viewpoint, Taylor (1984: 391) directs our attention to an important fact:

> Students typically read articles very quickly and promptly begin to compose, while successful writers insert a second step of thinking. Successful writers are aware that they might misinterpret the article. They might misread an important passage and draw incorrect conclusions, they monitor whether they are reading into or adding to what the author has said and check their ideas with the text.

This is also true for abstracting and the dangers of reading superficially considerably strengthens the need for inserting a second or (sometimes) a third reading phase into the process.

When we speak about the role of reading in the abstracting process, we have to be aware of the circumstance that it is difficult to distinguish between reading and analysing, as they occur virtually at the same time and may be identical (Taylor, 1984). It is also necessary to understand that reading and comprehension (text understanding) are two closely related phenomena (Pinto, 1994). We will cover this in more detail in the subsection on comprehension in Chapter 7. The main characteristics of the general reading process are described by Pinto et al. (2005) as follows. Reading is a process of intelligent visual perception aimed at decoding and comprehending the information contained in texts. Reading results in some kind of comprehension, which is a mental representation of the sense that we perceive from the text.

Good readers have to have an ample vocabulary and good knowledge of grammar. Enthusiasm in reading is also needed (Cremmins, 1982). Other factors that influence the reading process include the following:

- objectives;
- general world knowledge;
- background knowledge about the given topic;
- scholarly background;
- command of languages;
- command of the vocabulary;
- the ability to use strategies of analysis and synthesis;
- the type of text, its length and organisation;
- time available for reading;
- reading speed. (Pinto et al., 2005)

Reading is also very much directed by the following factors:

- the length of the words (longer words are easier to perceive than shorter ones);
- the familiarity of the words (unfamiliar words attract attention more easily);
- deliberate visual effects (headings, illustrations, tables, italicised words, etc.). Skilled abstractors can perceive and handle two or three such signs (Farrow, 1991).

Making sense

Reading is an interaction between reader and text. Thus readers create meaning, relying on textual clues and on their expectations. There are no ready-made meanings to be discovered and meanings will never be complete and explicit. Reading, nonetheless, is adequate for the given purpose. This requires creativity that characterises not only reading but is a prerequisite of the interpretation of any discourse (Widdowson, 1979).

It is not difficult to see that there are a number of similarities with abstracting here, while the differences lie in the communicative intent and readers' expectations. We know that abstractors are 'pre-reading' the original on behalf of the user (Collison, 1971). This means that they read the text and discover its meaning for the purpose of writing abstracts. Readers' expectation are thus not their own, but the expectations of the target audience, that is the users of the abstract. The meanings constructed during reading serve the purpose of finding relevant information. In this way, they are adequate for the given purpose.

We have to add that, in the case of abstracting, the abstract's target audience is broader than that for the original (Staiger, 1965). On the other hand, the targeted audience is relatively well known but far from homogeneous. It consists of the professionals of the given field (Endres-Niggemeyer, 1998).

Critical reading

We have already mentioned that there is a strong connection between information literacy and abstracting and that it is critical reading which acquires special importance in it. What we said in the subsection entitled 'The information literacy context' in Chapter 4 could be supplemented with a series of questions that provide both a general orientation and a critical approach if asked before starting to read:

- Who?
- When?
- What?

- For what reason?
- How?
- For what purpose?
- For whom? (Werlich, 1988)

Notwithstanding this, besides the similarities between reading critically in general and reading for the purpose of abstracting, there are a number of differences as well. This can be illustrated as follows. Critical thinkers recognise that reading uses one particular and limited perspective on a subject. They understand, consequently, that considering other perspectives is beneficial. They also read with a healthy scepticism, but do not doubt or deny what they read until they understand it (Paul, 1993).

In the abstracting context, scepticism seems to be of lesser importance in the sense that abstractors deal with texts that have already gone through some kind of quality control, usually peer review. This does not mean that abstractors cannot reject the ideas found in an article. In this case, the best solution is not to write an abstract on the given article. We have already pointed out in Chapter 3 that this might be a reasonable solution for expressing criticism instead of writing a critical abstract.

Techniques

The most useful reading techniques are those of reading for scientific research and reading for documentation purposes. Reading in general is far from being a homogeneous operation that is carried out with the same care and the same rhythm. We need to understand that if we do not read a text word by word, it is not negligent reading. Even full reading does not demand the same effort every time. It depends on the language, depth of content, difficulty and reading proficiency.

Reading *for scientific research* is immersive and critical. The parts of the text that discuss known facts in known ways, however, are not read but are only skimmed. Thus reading is selective and only selected parts of the text are read thoroughly. We do not, however, memorise them, but take notes instead. Reading *for documentation purposes* is similar in the sense that it is not a full reading of the whole text either. It means reading those parts of the text that contain information beyond the known facts and data, indicate new methods and results (Polzovics, 1962). Cremmins (1982) speaks about analytical reading, mainly in the same sense. He adds that analytical reading is present both actively for information content and passively for comprehension. He also differentiates between three stages of analytical reading as follows:

- retrieval reading, when the abstractor rapidly reads the original in order to identify the main content;
- creative reading, when the abstractor rereads the selected parts of the text;
- critical reading, when the abstractor reads the abstract for editing.

Reading and writing

Summarising may be seen as the junction where reading and writing take place (Uso and Palmer, 1998). Writers are devoted to the task of turning ideas into text. They then read the text to form new ideas and to make decisions about what has to be written and how should it be organised. Reflecting on texts includes information seeking as an analytic activity (Attfield et al., 2003). In consequence, looking for information, reading and writing are not independent of each other. Rather they happen at the same time and are constrained by one another in a complex way (Kwan, 2008). Writing is a complex web that comprises two major groups of processes, the first concerning the information needed for writing while the second involves reorganising this information into textual form. The first group involves collecting and connecting, where collecting means the assembly of information for writing, partially through reading. Connecting involves the sub-processes of selecting, ordering, discriminating and ranking the significance of the collected information, synthesising old with new information, and determining the need for further information. Reading means reviewing one's own text, in the sense that the writer reads almost simultaneously what has just been written (Murray, 1980).

How to evaluate abstracts

It is widely recognised that, despite the elusive nature of information quality, the quality of abstracts can be judged by the satisfaction of their intended users (Montesi and Urdiciain, 2005b; Pinto and Lancaster, 1999). Notwithstanding this, there are a number of external measures both quantitative and qualitative in nature.

Readability

The readability of an abstract is determined by the ability of the abstractors to express themselves in a clear, concise and unambiguous way. This requires the abstract to show a sufficient extent of cohesion and coherence (Pinto and Lancaster, 1999).

Readability is a formal, quantitative measure that uses formulae based on counting the number of syllables per word and measuring sentence length. There are a number of such formulae, for example:

- the Flesch Reading Ease Score;
- the Gunning Fog Index;
- the Flesh-Kincaid Grade Level.

The Flesch Reading Ease Score is perhaps the best known. In its original form, it corresponds to the following equation:

$$R.E. = 206.835 - 0.846w - 1.015s$$

where w = the average number of syllables per 100 words and s = the average number of words per sentence (Hartley et al., 2003).

The suitability of these formulae for effectively measuring text difficulty has been repeatedly questioned since the 1970s both in general and in relation to abstracting (Montesi and Urdiciain, 2005b). These formulae are not able to adequately capture the difficulty of a text if used exclusively. In addition to this, difficulty is much more an interaction between a text and the reader's capabilities than some innate property of a text (Yu, 2009). Despite these contradictions, readability measures have been used in several research studies. It seems, however, more suitable to use qualitative measures, even though qualitative investigations are much more difficult to conduct and quality is much more elusive than word counts and the like.

Qualitative measures

The evaluation of abstracts can be based on a number of quality factors. Of those described by Pinto and Lancaster (1999) the following are especially worthy of consideration:

- exhaustivity
- accuracy

- brevity
- density
- clarity.

Abstracts cannot include all the content of the original, only relevant pieces of information. This selection is based on the perceived needs of the particular audience. *Exhaustivity* measures to what extent abstracts include relevant information. Higher exhaustivity provides more access points to the contents of the original, making it more efficient in aiding retrieval.

Accuracy measures to what extent the information summarised is completely accurate and represents the original document faithfully. In some cases, abstractors are not fully familiar with the subject matter. Obscure original texts can also cause problems. If an original is in a language in which the abstractor is not completely fluent, the lower level of command is a source of misunderstandings. Besides that, a temporary lack of ability to concentrate that may be influenced by working conditions can result in a reduction in accuracy. Working under pressure, for example, when an abstractor may be required to produce a specified number of abstracts in a particular period also tends to lower accuracy (Pinto and Lancaster, 1999).

From all our previous argument it is clear (we could say even axiomatic) that abstracts are considerably shorter than original documents. *Brevity* is thus a well-known and desirable attribute of good abstracts (Pinto and Lancaster, 1999). Brevity can be achieved by reducing the redundancy which is a characteristic of all languages (Borko and Bernier, 1975). However, we can only do this to a certain extent because a lack of redundancy can impede reading comprehension since an unduly low level of redundancy decreases the predictability of the meaning of a message. Despite its importance, brevity is secondary to exhaustivity and accuracy. An examination of 11 database producers' guidelines, for example, did not reveal an instance where more emphasis would be given to the length of abstracts than to the importance of the content and the need to adequately reflect that content (Armstrong and Wheatley, 1998).

Density is a coefficient of the brevity and exhaustivity of the abstract – provided that all relevant information is included. As the length of the abstract lessens, its density grows, provided that the quantity of information remains constant. As we pointed out in Chapter 3, density is also a property of the original that influences the length of the abstract.

Clarity measures readability and intelligibility of the abstract in a qualitative way and depends on the abstractor's use of language. It includes the vocabulary and the grammatical structure of the abstract (Pinto and Lancaster, 1999).

All these quality factors can be correlated to the aspects of evaluation established by Koltay (1999):

1. Is there enough important information included in the abstract? This is a question about exhaustivity.

2. Are there unnecessary details included? This is the reverse of exhaustivity.

3. What is the level of abstraction? The level of abstraction is closely related to density and is a correlation of enough and unnecessary information.

4. Are there any misunderstandings (misrepresentations)? This question stresses accuracy.

5. How well is it formed in the target language? This equates to clarity.

The first two questions related to the inclusion of enough important information or of unnecessary details can be termed lack of information and excess of information respectively. These are qualities about which users have clear expectations (Montesi and Urdiciain, 2005b).

These questions can be supplemented by additional ones taken from the checklist provided by Cremmins (1982) for editors of abstracts. Compared to the above list, some of these questions bring in new points of view while others point towards more detail on a given issue. The questions are as follows:

- Is the abstract properly structured?
- Is the content of the abstract complete and concise?
- Is the abstract coherent?
- Does the abstract conform to the general style rules and conventions?
- Does the abstract conform to the specific requirements set up by the abstracting service?

Other considerations

Quality is not only a property of abstracts as products, but can be defined from the perspective of the user. To achieve this, Montesi and Urdiciain (2005b) carried out a series of interviews, the purpose of which was to find out as many problems as possible that abstracts might cause for potential users. They randomly selected a set of 60 traditional non-structured abstracts from six different Internet bibliographic databases (10 each). These databases covered education and agriculture. Sixty-two interviews were conducted in six European universities located in three countries: the Netherlands, Italy and Spain.

Several issues were identified, from which we selected the following:

- terminology;

- coherence;
- the density of abstracts.

The problems related to terminology appeared when users considered it:

- inaccurate and imprecise;
- incomprehensible or difficult;
- ambiguous;
- questionable.

With regard to the density of the abstracts, certain users complained about over-condensation of information in abstracts that resulted in a lack of clarity.

Montesi and Urdiciain (2005b: 520) also point out that '[in the abstracts studied] there were more complaints regarding a lack of information than an excess, since users could always skip redundant or uninteresting passages'.

We earlier defined the abstract as a cohesive and coherent text. Montesi and Urdiciain (2005b) found, however, that coherence could be lacking in some abstracts that they studied. Lack of coherence usually occurs at the end of the abstract, 'when something unexpected appears, and not even sound knowledge of the subject can help to decipher meaning' (Montesi and Urdiciain, 2005b: 522). Their study shows that abstract users start to read or to scan an abstract guided by expectations of, among other things, coherence.

The users expected to find topics mentioned earlier in the final parts of a given abstract. They looked back to locate a referent or referents that could explain why these words or phrases appeared. If they were unable to find them, they evidenced a flaw in the overall coherence of the abstract. Any failure to satisfy readers' expectations affected coherence, as they could not find the elements they considered 'necessary to build a comprehensive representation of the research, or ascertain the relevance of the research in its entirety or in part' (Montesi and Urdiciain, 2005b: 522).

The practice of abstracting: examples

The examples below show how the theoretical knowledge presented in the previous chapters can be used in practice. Before examining two texts and demonstrating some of the steps involved in writing abstracts based on these originals, it is worth having a look at an example of the worst practices in abstract writing provided by Hughes (2006), almost like a parody:

> *This paper discusses research, which was undertaken in the author's country. A theoretical framework is developed from a literature search and this is used by the authors as the basis of an analytical model. The researchers collected data within this framework and analysed it according to the precepts laid down by earlier researchers in the field. The data is used to demonstrate that our understanding can be significantly increased and this is discussed in the light of previous work. Conclusions are drawn and it is shown that these may be useful for practitioners.*

It is to be hoped that the abstracts which result from the following exercises do not fall within the category of bad abstracting as illustrated above but, on the contrary, demonstrate how to write useable abstracts.

Examples of abstract writing

We have chosen two texts, both written by the author. The motives behind selecting these two papers are manifold. First of all, these texts with all their virtues and vices are obviously close to me. Second, the topic of both texts is close to the reader of this book. I mention this in second place – and not by accident. Being close to our readership has both advantages and disadvantages. This is especially true for the first example, where the topic of the writing is abstracting. This makes the comprehension of the text easier, though the fact that the text of the example is about the same problem as the main text of the book may be slightly unsettling.

It is for this reason that we have distinguished the texts for analysis from other parts of the book. Not only do the numbered lines help with this but they are meant to ease the process of following the analysis. Thus we will refer to these numbers in the explanatory text.

A word about the second text: it is about writing proposals. Thus this topic may be less familiar and less confusing to the reader.

Example 1

In this example we analyse an article entitled 'Including Technical and Academic Writing in Translation Curricula' (Koltay, 1998, used by permission). The analysis is followed by a draft abstract, then an edited version of it supplemented with comments. Do not forget that the article itself is mainly about abstracting!

The original text

1 **Including Technical and Academic Writing in Translation Curricula**

2 Why should we include 'writing about a technical subject,
3 intended to convey specific information to a specific audience for
4 a specific purpose' (Markel, 1988) in a translation curriculum?
5 The reasons seem to be simple and obvious. Technical Writing
6 and Academic Writing, which in my opinion both correspond to the
7 above definition, widen translation students' professional
8 horizons. It allows them to become acquainted with the
9 characteristics of a number of new genres and equips them with
10 the necessary skills to produce texts corresponding to these
11 genres. By designing a number of assignments in which they have
12 to decide what is really important in a text and what is not, writing
13 instruction can be formed in such a way that students
14 concentrate on the notion of the importance of information.

15 Introduction to scholarly communication is also a great benefit.
16 Activities and documents related to organising a conference,
17 publishing scholarly papers, etc. are a novelty for the majority of
18 students. On the other hand, translators may very well be
19 engaged in such activities as often they are in a given workplace
20 the only persons equipped with substantial language skills. (At
21 least this is the situation in Hungary.) Encounters with new texts
22 also develop the student's vocabulary in the target language.

23 Benefits are especially visible if we speak about an important
24 genre: abstracting. Palmer and Uso enumerate the benefits of
25 abstracting in connection with teaching English as a second
26 language. I believe that these benefits are also valid if we teach
27 abstracting to students of translation (who by the way often
28 regard their training as an enhanced form of language learning).
29 The benefits of abstracting are in turn mostly applicable to the
30 entire spectrum of writing instruction.

31 By teaching our students how to write abstracts we will
32 enhance their reading and writing ability, engaging them in an
33 activity that is communicative and in which students apply
34 knowledge previously acquired (Uso and Palmer, 1998).

35 Abstracting not only employs decoding and encoding and
36 develops critical reading skills, but it enhances the understanding of
37 basic rhetorical principles. As some texts are not perfect, students
38 will discover flawed patterns while abstracting (Guinn, 1979).

39 **The case of Professional Documentation**

40 Professional Documentation (PD) is a course designed to make
41 students of translation acquainted with those written genres of
42 linguistic (interlingual) mediation, that are not translation, but
43 which a translator may be required to write. PD is part of the
44 technical translation curriculum at the Technical University of
45 Budapest. This programme contains courses preparing future
46 translators for jobs that go beyond the boundaries of pure
47 translation. The education of translators began at TUB in 1990.
48 First, there was a course in English translation only. German
49 translation was introduced in 1991, French and Russian in 1993.
50 The total administrative, subject and examination system
51 framework of the three-year training has been established.
52 Curricula as well as syllabuses have become standardised
53 according to the same principles applying to the courses in all
54 four languages.

55 Despite standardisation, there are differences in available
56 teaching materials in different languages, and the languages
57 themselves require different approaches to PD. That is why the
58 description below will be limited to PD for students of English
59 translation.

60 Translators are trained in a six-semester postgraduate course.
61 Applicants for the programme have to take an entry examination.
62 Ten subjects are taught in the entire course, and the classes take
63 eight to ten hours a week per semester. These time limits are
64 imposed by the fact that the course can only be taken as a minor
65 or supplementary degree course so as to allow students to
66 complete it simultaneously with their major professional training
67 course.

68 The only six-semester course is English language. Written
69 translation begins only in the second semester. Among other
70 subjects the students have courses in their native Hungarian
71 language, the cultural and economic background of the target
72 (foreign) language, stylistics and terminology of technical
73 language.

74 PD begins in the fifth semester and it is a one-hour course
75 through the sixth semester. It is taught in the same semesters as
76 *Technical Style and Terminology*, which provides linguistic
77 background knowledge for technical translation and interpretation
78 as well as other types of linguistic transfer activity. In the third

79 year there is *Negotiation Practice*, which is the oral counterpart of
80 PD, dealing with oral transfer other than interpretation.
81   Aside from the preceding courses *Contrastive and Functional*
82 *Grammar* has to be mentioned. Introduced in the second year of
83 the training, it summarises and consolidates the grammar skills
84 related to Hungarian and the foreign language on the basis of
85 universal semantic functions.
86   Due to the recent trends in student mobility and the increase
87 in the diversity of essential professional skills, students and
88 graduates of other universities are now also admitted to these
89 courses. As a consequence, there is a great variety of interests
90 and professional experience within each student group, which has
91 to be taken into consideration in order to make the training
92 effective.
93   The main topics covered in the course are the following.

94 ■ The concept and content of Professional Documentation
95 ■ Instructions and manuals
96 ■ Scholarly and professional societies
97 ■ Scientific conferences
98 ■ Report writing
99 ■ Scientific literature
100 ■ The scientific paper
101 ■ Writing abstracts.

102 The last topic assumes special importance as at TUB the state
103 examination, which concludes the education of technical
104 translators, includes abstract writing as we consider abstracting
105 to be an important skill. Thus an abstract of a technical article in
106 English has to be prepared in Hungarian.
107   In PD the most typical working method is to analyse English
108 texts in Hungarian and then produce similar documents in English
109 or in Hungarian depending on the genre. The main emphasis is
110 on the content of the documents and good style in Hungarian as
111 in the majority of cases students' documents are written in
112 Hungarian.
113   The very first class begins with a discussion with students
114 about the *content of PD*. Even though this is a short discussion,
115 many students have a good idea of the content of the course.

116   In the final two years we try to give more attention to the
117   problems of writing *instructions and manuals*. This is the 'most
118   technical' topic that is often mentioned in the discussion about
119   the content of PD. Text and exercises in Markel's textbook (Markel,
120   1988) are put to good use here. Students analyse efficiency of
121   instructions given in the book (especially in exercise 2 on page
122   237). They write simple instructions choosing from a list given in
123   exercise 1, but they perform this latter exercise in Hungarian. The
124   students most frequently choose the following topics:

125   ■ How to load film into a 35 mm camera
126   ■ How to change a bicycle tyre
127   ■ How to parallel-park a car.

128   The problem of documents related to the functioning of *learned*
129   *societies* is closely connected to the topic of instructions. Namely
130   we analyse a 'How to Start' type booklet prepared by a
131   professional society that is very close to a short manual though
132   it has different aims. After a classroom discussion the students
133   are required to make an adapted translation of this text. They
134   have to leave out everything that is untypical for Hungary and they
135   can rewrite part of the information contained in the original
136   according to the different situation. Nonetheless, this exercise is
137   the one that requires the students to make the most use of their
138   translating skills.
139   For this exercise we use a booklet of the American Society of
140   Indexers *How to Start Indexing*. Our students may not be
141   interested in becoming indexers, even though subject specialists
142   with language (translation) skills often do become abstractors
143   and indexers. Nonetheless we are not interested in the
144   profession itself but in the way the professional society delivers
145   its message. *How to Start Indexing* is a short, easy-to-understand
146   text that fulfils its function of providing information about the
147   profession. On the other hand it contains information on training
148   courses and gives advice on charging for the work done. Both are
149   different in Hungary, thus the students have to adapt their text to
150   the reality in our country. For example, training courses related to
151   indexing have differing names from those in the United States
152   and can be attended not only in library schools but at the National
153   Széchényi Library.

154   The nature of PD often lends itself to the use of role-playing,
155   which is not direct oral role-playing, but writing imaginary
156   documents.

157   One example of role-playing is the *Call for Papers* exercise. The
158   students become acquainted with a good example of this genre,
159   then they have to write one for any fictitious conference, seminar,
160   etc. This exercise results in a Call for Papers written in English.
161   Writing is preceded by a short discussion of the importance of
162   conferences and the main organisational steps that have to be
163   taken. Examining a Call for Papers gives one an opportunity to
164   explain what a plenary session, a round-table, etc. are. The main
165   goal is not translation, but to be able to produce a Call for Papers
166   in English. Nonetheless, we identify the Hungarian equivalents of
167   the technical terms used in this field.

168   One good example of real-life texts used for this exercise is the
169   Call for Papers issued for the Fifth Congress of the International
170   Association for Semiotic Studies held in Berkeley, CA. This Call for
171   Papers is a good example of this genre, which – on the other
172   hand – shows a number of features that would not be
173   characteristic in other environments. Participants, for example,
174   could make use of a special accommodation package, as the
175   conference was held on a university campus. There was another
176   special feature in this document as well. Beside the usual
177   submission of abstracts, a condensed form of abstracts had to
178   be produced to allow for the large number of papers to be
179   presented in written form at the conference. This feature is less
180   typical at a number of other conferences.

181   Thus, on the one hand, this document represents a possible
182   model for a Call for Papers. On the other hand, it directs the
183   students' attention to the fact that any similar model should be
184   adapted to local circumstances.

185   It is the first time during the course that the students come
186   across the word 'abstract'. At this stage we do not explain in
187   detail what an abstract is, but remind them that it will play an
188   important role in our course and will be dealt with extensively.

189   *Report writing* is learned using a workbook that the students
190   can fill in on their own. This workbook has been designed for
191   students of De Montfort University, Great Britain. Its main
192   objectives are to enable students to 'recognise and understand
193   the report format as distinct from essays and other written styles'

194 and to design and organise a good report structure (Hilton,
195 1995).

196 Reports are in many respects similar in their structure to
197 *scientific papers*, so the knowledge acquired with the former can
198 be transferred to the latter. To get a better understanding of the
199 requirements of a scientific paper we examine a number of
200 instructions for authors taken from different scientific journals.

201 Even though they are referred to by different names in different
202 journals, these are instructions. The students – as mentioned
203 earlier – have already learned how to prepare them. This time we
204 use them in 'the opposite direction' as a basis for the discovery
205 of structural patterns in scholarly papers.

206 The students will learn that a typical scientific article shows a
207 structure that corresponds to one of the varieties of the
208 'Introduction – Methods – Results – Discussion – Conclusions
209 (IMRD/IMRC)' scheme. They have to know that this is less typical
210 in the case of social sciences and humanities, popular science
211 articles, magazine articles, etc. To strengthen their knowledge,
212 the students have to take a scientific paper in English of their
213 choice and label its main formal and structural elements. In
214 addition to this, they have to write a short paper corresponding to
215 the IMRD structure on any real or imaginary topic in Hungarian (or,
216 if they wish, in English).

217 The knowledge of an article's structure is useful as well when
218 we begin to deal with *abstracting*. Students know that most
219 documents contain background information, as well as
220 descriptions of well-known techniques, equipment, processes and
221 results, which should be omitted in the abstract.

222 Abstracting classes begin with reading a short passage, taken
223 from the Career Guide of Neufeld and Cornog as a kind of motivation
224 and confrontation with reality. This passage explains that abstracting
225 is a series of small challenges: no two are alike, yet the writing must
226 be consistent, accurate and finished on time. The abstractor should
227 also enjoy the challenge of reducing the work to its essentials. A
228 creative, detective-like skill is needed to find the main points in a
229 wordy, poorly written article (Neufeld and Cornog, 1983).

230 It is important to explain English terminology, even if students
231 write the abstracts in Hungarian. Students must know that there
232 is a conceptual difference between 'summaries' and abstracts
233 and that informative abstracts are often called 'descriptive'.

234   Nonetheless terminology does not need to be overemphasised.
235   We dedicate the most attention to writing informative abstracts. It
236   is widely recognised that it is relatively easy to write indicative
237   abstracts, while it is very hard to produce informative ones
238   (Manning, 1990).

239   Students are already familiar with the notion of the abstract in
240   different contexts. They see that at a congress an abstract is
241   required before a paper is accepted. They have to know that this
242   is a pre-text ('unfinished', 'promissory') text that will be elaborated
243   into a full text (Gläser, 1995).

244   The topics we deal with in the classes on abstracting are the
245   following:

246   ■ The notion of the abstract
247   ■ The functions abstracts have to fulfil
248   ■ Types of abstracts
249   ■ Informative
250   ■ Indicative
251   ■ Mixed
252   ■ The abstracting process and its rules.

253   Along with the well-known features of *informative abstracts* we
254   direct the students' attention to the fact that informative
255   abstracts concentrate on what the original says, retaining in
256   condensed form the inherent thinking of the original (Guinn,
257   1979), while indicative abstracts always contain some kind of
258   (often implicit) reference to the original (Kuhlen, 1984). This
259   means that the informative abstract is created in a way that is
260   hardly different from an original text. Similarity is even more
261   evident if we disregard in the abstract the identification of the
262   source, the (optional) signature or initials of the abstractor, etc.,
263   which show its secondary nature. The students learn that
264   translating the author's abstracts found in the original does not
265   produce in most cases a satisfactory abstract in the target
266   language.

267   Exercises include looking for topic sentences in texts,
268   analysing text structures and the headings of scientific articles
269   along with other types of texts. We analyse the appropriate
270   theoretical passages of technical writing textbooks (Damerst and

271 Bell, 1990; Lannon, 1990; Rutherford, 1991). The students have
272 to read these texts critically, comparing them to each other and
273 to the short lecture they receive on the main issues of
274 abstracting.

275 We use the textbooks not only for acquiring theoretical
276 knowledge but to do some exercises before we begin to write
277 informative abstracts (which is the most important activity in the
278 abstracting part of PD).

279 This can be illustrated using the example of Lannon's book
280 (pp. 140–50). After analysing the theoretical part, we examine
281 the checklist that highlights a number of important steps in the
282 abstracting process. We do not only use the checklist. Lannon's
283 book provides a detailed example of summarising a text. This
284 exercise shows the steps taken and tools used during the
285 summary process and has proved very useful for our students.
286 We imagine that our work is to produce a newsletter summary on
287 the topic of municipal trash incinerators. We follow up in groups
288 by examining the result of deleting questionable points, including
289 key findings, etc. We examine how all these appear in the final
290 draft and the trimmed-down version of the abstract.

291 We discuss here how important it is to give attention to cultural
292 differences when abstracting into a different language. Hungarian
293 readers, for example, may be familiar with the problems and
294 lawsuits resulting from the use of Agent Orange during the
295 Vietnam War. Most probably they do not know what happened at
296 Love Canal, while the name of Seveso sounds to them fairly
297 familiar. All this has to be taken into account when selecting the
298 best possible dioxin-related example.

299 The revision checklist at the end of this chapter shows an
300 obvious difference between intra-lingual and inter-lingual
301 abstracting. The question 'Is it written in correct English?' is
302 senseless if the target language is Hungarian.

303 The abstract produced in this exercise is meant for a relatively
304 wide and non-professional audience, while the main aim of the
305 abstracting classes of course is to teach how to write abstracts
306 for professionals. We direct the students' attention to this
307 difference and to the fact that the varied needs of different
308 audiences will play an important role in our course.

309 After using textbooks, we go to 'real texts'. One of the most
310 problematic parts of the classes is to determine the intended

311 audience of the abstract (or any other text) to be prepared. Much
312 flexibility is needed here.
313   For example, the students are allowed to write longer abstracts
314 or abstracts that contain more details from the original. This is
315 possible if they can define their intended readers and can argue
316 that a longer explanation is necessary for a less professionally
317 oriented readership.
318   It is also difficult to find actual scientific texts that would show
319 the above typical structure and would be understandable to all
320 students. Thus we use different texts and when they do not
321 correspond to the IMRD/IMRC structure, we make the students
322 aware of that. Also we can use the texts selected for the abstract-
323 writing exercise from the examinations in previous years.
324   The most important activity, i.e. abstract writing itself, is done
325 both with the teacher's assistance and independently.
326 Independent writing and group work are followed by analyses of
327 the work done and discussion of possible alternatives, mistakes
328 and their correction.
329   The abstracting exercises are graded using the following criteria:

330 ■ Is there enough important information included in the abstract?
331 ■ Are unnecessary details included?
332 ■ Are there any misunderstandings in the abstract?
333 ■ What is the level of abstraction?
334 ■ How well is it worded in Hungarian?

335 In the beginning we mentioned that we focus very much on
336 scholarly communication. For this reason a brief discussion on
337 the importance and the nature of scientific literature precedes
338 the classes dealing with its different genres. This discussion
339 includes a snapshot on the use of the Internet and its possible
340 influence on the future of writing.

341   **Bibliography**

342 Damerst, W. and Bell, A.H., *Clear Technical Communication*. San
343   Diego, CA: Harcourt Brace Jovanovic, 1990.
344 Gläser, R., Summarizing texts as genres of academic writing.
345   *Summarizing Text for Intelligent Communication. Dagstuhl*
346   *Seminar Report,* 1995, *http://www.bid.fh-hannover.de/SimSum/*
347   *Abstract/Abstracts/Glaser/Glaser.html.*

153

348 Guinn, D.M., Composing an abstract: a practical heuristic. *College*
349   *Composition and Communication*, 30(4), pp. 380–83, 1979.

350 Hilton, A., *Report Writing*. Study pack. Leicester: De Montfort
351   University Student Learning Development Centre, 1995.

352 Kuhlen, R., Some similarities and differences between intellectual
353   and machine text understanding for the purpose of
354   abstracting. *Representation and Exchange of Knowledge as a*
355   *Basis of Information Processes*. Amsterdam: Elsevier, 1984,
356   pp. 87–109.

357 Lannon, J.M., *Technical Writing*. 5th ed. Boston: Little, Brown,
358   1990.

359 Manning, A.D., Abstracts in relation to larger and smaller
360   discourse structures. *Journal of Technical Writing and*
361   *Communication*, 20(4), pp. 369–90, 1990.

362 Markel, M.H., *Technical Writing. Situations and Strategies*, 2nd
363   edn. New York: St. Martin's Press, 1988.

364 Neufeld, M.L. and Cornog, M., *Abstracting and Indexing: A Career*
365   *Guide*. Philadelphia: NFAIS, 1983.

366 Rutherford, A.J., *Basic Communication Skills*. Englewood Cliffs, NJ:
367   Prentice Hall, 1991.

368 Uso, E. and Palmer, J.C., A product-focused approach to text
369   summarisation. *The Internet TESL Journal*, IV(1), January
370   1998. *http://www.aitech.ac.jp/~iteslj/*.

Analysis

The analysed text contains 3,352 words (3,113 without references).

The text begins with a question 'Why should we ...' that has to be avoided in the abstract, even though this question does not repeat the title. Line 6 contains the words 'in my opinion'. This indicates that the author stresses that this is his personal opinion. In line 15 the word 'also' shows the beginning of a new topic: 'Introduction to scholarly communication is also a great benefit.' To repeat this sentence would be overly general. The actual concrete content is in the following sentences.

The clause 'by the way' in line 27 shows that the following content is secondary in the author's personal opinion. The statement that begins in line 29 touches upon the general context as it says, 'The benefits of abstracting are in turn mostly applicable to the entire spectrum of writing instruction.'

In line 40 a non-standard acronym is defined: 'Professional Documentation (PD)'. This acronym has to be included in the abstract, first in this form and then the abbreviation 'PD' can be used. The acronym 'TUB' is not defined in line 47 where it appears first, but in line 45.

The particle 'Despite' in line 55 directs our attention not only to the contrast between standards and other approaches. It also shows the importance of the passage: 'Despite standardisation, there are differences in available teaching materials in different languages, and the languages themselves require different approaches to PD.'

The section headed 'The case of Professional Documentation' that begins with line 39 consists of at least three parts. The first part is the definition of Professional Documentation (PD). As PD is relatively unknown, it is advisable to include some information about it in the abstract. The second part gives background information to PD, thus it should be treated cautiously in order not to include more details in the abstract beyond what is necessary. In the case of information on the history of PD that begins with line 47, the abstractor has to weigh up the pros and cons of including it in the abstract.

The sentences which begin with line 86 provide interesting details about the education of translators described in the article: 'Due to the recent trends in student mobility and the increase in the diversity of essential professional skills, students and graduates of other universities are now also admitted to these courses ...' This information, however, would most probably be left out from a 'standard' abstract.

The third part explains the content of PD. In this regard the bulleted list from line 94 serves as orientation. This and all subsequent bulleted lists have to be transformed into linear text.

The sentence 'The last topic assumes special importance' in line 102 indicates that the author attaches importance to the subsequent sentences, which are about abstracting. From these sentences we learn that they are important indeed. Abstracting is one of the subjects of the state examination and its importance is repeatedly expressed: 'we consider abstracting to be an important skill' (line 102).

Line 113 may seem interesting: 'The very first class begins with a discussion with students about the *content of PD.*' This sentence merely indicates that such a thing happens but does not provide any content. This is very much a sentence that would characterise an indicative abstract, except that it is in a primary document. It is not the task of the abstractor to judge the quality of the original. Nevertheless, we may agree that it is natural to begin a class with an introduction to the topics to be covered, even if it came about in a dialogical form (not mentioned in the text). Whatever we think about the appropriateness of such a sentence in the original, it is not needed in the abstract.

Line 107 contains one of the key sentences of the text that has to be included in the abstract: 'In PD the most typical working method is to analyse English texts in Hungarian and then produce similar documents in English or in Hungarian depending on the genre.' Its importance is indicated by the superlative of the adjective. For a shorter abstract, however, it could be judged a minor detail. Overall, a more detailed discussion of the topics of PD that are not related to abstracting could be part of a longer abstract. This consideration would depend on how much importance we attribute to abstracting within PD.

Line 208, where the IMRD structure is mentioned, provides a good example of how to apply the requirement of objectivity. We know that there is a close relationship between the structure of the original and that of the abstract. Still, this article does not explicitly mention this relationship, thus it should not figure in the abstract, even if there is a vague connection there, as the difficulty of finding appropriate texts that show the IMRD structure is mentioned in line 318.

The sentence, which begins with the words 'Abstracting classes begin with reading a short passage ...' (line 222) covers an interesting detail but it is highly unlikely that such a statement of detail would find place in an abstract that shows a proper level of abstraction.

As mentioned above, a longer abstract could contain more details, among which would be the content of the passage beginning with line 253 as well as that beginning on line 299.

Draft abstract

The first draft contains 634 words from selected passages. It still contains bulleted lists.

Professional Documentation (PD) is a course designed to make students of translation acquainted with those written genres of linguistic (interlingual) mediation that are not translation but which a translator may be required to write. PD is part of the technical translation curriculum at the Technical University of Budapest.
The main topics covered in the course are the following:

- the concept and content of Professional Documentation;
- instructions and manuals;

- scholarly and professional societies;
- scientific conferences;
- report writing;
- scientific literature;
- the scientific paper;
- writing abstracts.

The latter topic assumes special importance as at TUB the state examination which concludes the education of technical translators includes abstract writing as we consider abstracting to be an important skill. Thus an abstract of a technical article in English has to be prepared in Hungarian.

In PD the most typical working method is to analyse English texts in Hungarian and then produce similar documents in English or in Hungarian depending on the genre. It is important to explain English terminology, even if students write the abstracts in Hungarian. Students must know that there is a conceptual difference between 'summaries' and abstracts and that informative abstracts are often called 'descriptive'.

We dedicate the most attention to writing informative abstracts. It is widely recognised that it is relatively easy to write indicative abstracts while it is very hard to produce informative ones.

The topics we deal with in the classes on abstracting are the following:

- the notion of the abstract;
- the functions abstracts have to fulfil;
- types of abstracts;
- informative;
- indicative;
- mixed;
- the abstracting process and its rules.

Alongside the well-known features of *informative abstracts* we direct the students' attention to the fact that informative abstracts concentrate on what the original says, retaining in condensed form the inherent thinking of the original, while indicative abstracts always contain some kind of (often implicit) reference to the original. This means that the informative abstract is created in a way that is scarcely different from an original text. The similarity is even more evident if we disregard in the abstract the identification of the source and the (optional) signature or initials of the abstractor, etc., which show its secondary nature.

The students learn that translating the *author's abstracts* found in the original does not produce in most cases a satisfactory abstract in the target language.

Exercises include looking for topic sentences in texts, analysing text structures and the headings of scientific articles along with other types of texts. We analyse the appropriate theoretical passages of technical writing textbooks. The students have to read these texts critically and compare them to each other and to the short lecture they receive on the main issues of abstracting.

We discuss here how important it is to give attention to cultural differences when abstracting into a different language.

One of the most problematic parts of the classes is to determine the intended audience of the abstract (or any other text) to be prepared. Much flexibility is needed here.

It is also difficult to find actual scientific texts that would show the above typical structure and be understandable to all students. Thus we use different texts and when they do not correspond to the IMRD/IMRC structure, we make the students aware that this is so. Also we can use the texts selected for the abstract-writing exercise for the examinations in previous years.

The most important activity, i.e. abstract-writing itself, is done both with the teacher's assistance and independently.

The abstracting exercises are graded using the following criteria:

- Is there enough important information included in the abstract?
- Are unnecessary details included?
- Are there any misunderstandings in the abstract?
- What is the level of abstraction?
- How well is it worded in Hungarian?

The edited version

The edited version contains 223 words (in three paragraphs).

Professional Documentation (PD) is a course that makes students of translation acquainted with written genres of interlingual mediation that are not translation, but which a translator may be required to write. PD is part of the technical translation curriculum at the Technical University of Budapest. It covers, among other topics, instructions and manuals, report writing, scientific papers and abstracting. This last is part of the state examination: an abstract of a technical article in English has to be prepared in Hungarian. The most typical working method of PD is to analyse English texts in Hungarian and then produce similar documents in English or in Hungarian with the teacher's assistance and independently.

English terminology is explained without overemphasising it. The most attention is dedicated to writing informative abstracts, with special attention to the characteristics of informative abstracts, especially the existence of references to the original in indicative abstracts. Other topics dealt with are the notion, functions and types of abstracts, the abstracting process and its rules, and the need to treat author abstracts of the originals critically.

Exercises include looking for topic sentences in texts, analysing text structures and the headings of scientific articles along with other types of texts. Technical writing textbooks are used, though critically. The main difficulty is determining the intended audience of the abstracts and in finding actual scientific texts for abstracting.

Comments on the edited version

This abstract is extremely concise at a length of 223 words. Besides cutting the list that enumerates the topics of PD and using 'among other topics' we write 'abstracting' instead of 'abstract writing'. All this helps to save on the number of words.

The sentence 'The state examination includes abstract writing' had to be modified to produce a cohesive text. Its content did not change, only its structure. The state examination itself appears twice in the original. According to the rules, however, it is mentioned only once in the abstract. To connect this sentence more properly and strengthen cohesion and coherence, we changed the beginning of the sentence – from 'Abstracting is part of the state examination ...' to 'This last is part of the state examination ...' – as the sentence does not stand alone without connection to the previous part of the text, even at the cost of an extra word.

The sentence about English terminology was not included in the above draft. It is, nonetheless, an important part of the abstract.

The clause 'the need to treat author abstracts of the originals critically' does not figure in the original in this form. It reads as follows: 'The students learn that translating the author's abstracts found in the original does not produce in most cases a satisfactory abstract in the target language.' Besides the more economical wording, it uses the more correct term. Instead of 'author's abstracts', it uses 'author abstracts'.

There are a few details which could be included in a somewhat longer abstract. We could mention not only the existence of references in indicative abstracts, but also other characteristics of informative ones. There could be a place for the criteria for grading the abstracting exercises.

The sentence 'The most typical working method is to analyse English texts in Hungarian and then produce similar documents in English or in Hungarian with the teacher's assistance and independently' is made of two sentences that can be found in different places of the original: lines 107 and 325.

Example 2

As indicated earlier, the second example (Koltay, 2002, used by permission) is based on an article about teaching proposal writing to translators. It begins with a reflection on the framework of Professional Documentation mentioned in the first example. It also has a reference to that paper.

The original text

1   **Teaching Proposal Writing to Translators**

2 In an earlier paper published in *Translation Journal* (Koltay, 1998)
3 I argued for a genre-based writing education of translators. My
4 argument was that translators may be called upon to produce
5 different text genres in a given foreign language that go beyond
6 the scope of translation. This was the main reason for introducing
7 writing instruction into the education of translators at the
8 Budapest University of Technology and Economics (formerly the
9 Technical University of Budapest) in 1992.
10   The course where written genres of linguistic (interlingual)
11 mediation are addressed is called Professional Documentation
12 (PD). It contains elements of both technical and academic writing.
13   The reasons for teaching PD are manifold. Besides providing
14 insight into a number of important and interesting genres, PD is
15 a good general exercise that widens students' professional
16 horizons. Moreover, translators are specialised writers. Thus
17 getting acquainted with written texts and producing them helps
18 the students to become better translators.
19   I agree with Eileen Brockbank (2001), who explains in *Translation*
20 *Journal* that a translator's most important skill is writing – in the
21 target language.
22   One of the genres such writing education can make use of is
23 the proposal. Proposals represent a genre that is highly useful for
24 any writer, including translators. Well-written proposals multiply
25 the chances of being accepted. In many cases proposals have to
26 be prepared in two or more languages. Translators familiar with
27 the genre and the cultural differences between the source and the

28 target language can render a highly useful service. This is true
29 even if we know that proposals differ by their type and conditions
30 of their submission.
31   As we will see, proposal writing is strongly related to
32 extralingual information. The importance of extralingual factors is
33 a fact that not only influences practical activities, but has also
34 been acknowledged by theoreticians. Semiotic Textology, e.g. as
35 laid out by Békési, Petőfi and Vass (1999), not only uses strictly
36 formal, linguistic analysis, but supplements it with methodologies
37 that are capable of operating with encyclopaedic (world)
38 knowledge. It investigates the competencies of the sender and
39 the receiver, their relationship and their dominant intentions in
40 communicative situations.
41   Coming back to proposals, in the most general terms, a written
42 proposal is a document in which the writer offers something
43 beneficial to the reader in exchange for something in return.
44   The writer (or writers and the organisation they represent) may
45 offer to conduct research, develop systems, design and build
46 equipment, improve services, repair damage, increase profits,
47 etc. In return, the reader (or readers and the organisation they
48 represent) will provide funding, payment, equipment and other
49 support.
50   The proposal may reflect a need recognised and stated by the
51 reader, by the writer, or both. This gives us the foundations for a
52 typology of proposals.
53   Not all, but most, proposals fall into the following six categories:

54 ■   applications for government grants;
55 ■   bids for government contracts;
56 ■   applications for foundation grants;
57 ■   applications for corporate grants;
58 ■   bids for commercial contracts;
59 ■   internal proposals (where writer and reader are members of
60   the same organisation). (Haselkorn, 1985)

61 Proposals are often written according to the requirements set out
62 in Requests for Proposals (RFPs).
63   Proposals are delivered to a specific audience to achieve a
64 specific purpose. The audience of a proposal may include both

65 technical and non-technical readers. Both groups have to be
66 addressed. One part of the audience may be interested in the
67 results, another part in the costs, and again others in trying out
68 new things. Some may resist new ideas. The following questions
69 have to be answered concerning the audience of a proposal:

70 ■ Who is the real audience?
71 ■ What does the reader already know?
72 ■ What does the reader want to know?
73 ■ What does the reader not want to know?
74 ■ What does the reader perceive?

75 The person (or persons) who can make a decision or take action
76 as a result of the proposal constitutes the real audience. In many
77 cases there are many readers of a proposal. The first reader may
78 have the authority to reject the idea but not the authority to
79 approve it. A proposal may be evaluated by a team selected for
80 that purpose. A good proposal should include information
81 necessary to have each person who receives it take the
82 appropriate action, as well as information required to ensure that
83 the right person sees it. From this perspective, the audience can
84 be divided into three distinct categories:

85 ■ Primary audience – the person or persons who can make
86 decisions or act on the proposal.
87 ■ Secondary audience – those who will be affected by the
88 decision or action taken.
89 ■ Intermediate audience – those who review and route the
90 proposal.

91 Individual readers often tend to focus on their own areas of
92 interest and specialisation. Some of them focus on technical
93 details, others on budgetary and financial matters, and those who
94 work in personnel may focus primarily on the way people will be
95 influenced (Bowman and Branchaw, 1992).
96 A linguistic analysis of research grant proposals submitted to
97 the European Union (Connor and Mauranen, 1999) showed that,
98 following the model for article introductions proposed by Swales
99 (1990), ten rhetorical moves can be identified. Of these moves

100   the following nine occur in the majority of proposals:

101   ■ Establishing territory
102   ■ Gap
103   ■ Goal
104   ■ Means
105   ■ Reporting previous research
106   ■ Achievements
107   ■ Benefits
108   ■ Competence claim
109   ■ Importance claim.

110   The first move in most proposals examined was one which
111   established the territory in which the research placed itself. They
112   found that it is possible to distinguish two types of territory, of
113   which at least one but sometimes both were used:

114   ■ a 'real-world' territory, i.e. how the proposed project is
115   situated in the world outside the research field;
116   ■ a research territory, i.e. the field of research within the
117   discipline or disciplines of the project.

118   The *Gap* move indicates that there is a gap in knowledge or a
119   problem in the territory. The gap move is again very similar to the
120   second Swalesian introduction move known as 'establishing a
121   niche'. Like the territorial move, the gap can also be placed either
122   in the 'real world' (for instance environmental, commercial or
123   financial problems), or in the research world (for example pointing
124   out that something is not known or not known with certainty, or
125   needs to be known).
126   An important aspect of this move is placing one's work in
127   relation to the consensus in the field. The researcher needs to be
128   innovative, yet the proposed research has to remain within the
129   constraints of the field. Citation of sources helps a great deal in
130   solving this dilemma.
131   The *Goal* move is a statement of the aim or general objective
132   of the study. Depending on its formulation, the real-world element
133   may be present or the research territory element may dominate.

134 The *Means* move specifies how the goal will be achieved. This
135 move describes the methods, procedures, plans of action and
136 tasks that are to lead to the goal.

137 The *Reporting previous research* move consists of reporting or
138 referring to earlier research in the field, either by the proposers
139 themselves or by others.

140 Using the *Achievements* move, the proposals present their
141 anticipated results, findings or outcomes of the study.

142 The *Benefits* move comprises intended or projected outcomes
143 of the study, presented in terms of their usefulness and value to
144 the world outside, the study itself or the domain of research in
145 itself.

146 The *Competence claim* move introduces the research group or
147 its responsible members. It makes a statement to the effect that
148 the research group is well qualified, experienced and generally
149 capable of carrying out the tasks it proposes to undertake.

150 The *Importance claim* move makes out the proposal, its
151 objectives, anticipated outcomes or the territory as particularly
152 important or topical, much needed or urgent with respect to either
153 the 'real world' or to the research field.

154 No matter how persuasive the tone of the proposal, it may be
155 rejected. In general terms, proposals are rejected because of:

156 (a) No trust – for one reason or another, the reader does not trust
157   the writers, their organisation, or members of the given
158   profession in general.

159 (b) No need – the reader doesn't perceive a problem.

160 (c) No desire – the reader perceives a problem but doesn't
161   believe that it is sufficiently important to worry about.

162 (d) No urgency – the reader perceives a problem and would like
163   it solved but has higher priorities at the moment.

164 (e) No value – the reader perceives a problem and would like it
165   to be solved, but doesn't believe that the proposed solution
166   will provide an adequate return on investment.

167   (Bowman and Branshaw, 1992)

168 This list shows well the differences between solicited and
169 unsolicited proposals. If we prepare a solicited proposal, it is
170 unlikely that it would be rejected under (b) or (c). Obviously the
171 reader's perception depends on how detailed and unambiguous

166

172   the RFP was. This is also true in the case of (d). 'No trust' may
173   be the case regardless of whether the proposal is solicited or
174   unsolicited.
175   Beside this, it is useful to consider the following, more detailed
176   list of possible causes for rejection.

177   1.   The proposer did not demonstrate a clear understanding of
178   the problem.
179   2.   The proposal did not arrive by the submission deadline.
180   3.   The information requested in the RFP was not provided.
181   4.   The objectives were not well defined.
182   5.   The wrong audience was addressed.
183   6.   The procedures and methodology were not specific.
184   7.   The overall design was questionable.
185   8.   The proposal lacked evidence of intent to meet all terms and
186   conditions specified in the RFP.
187   9.   Cost estimates were not realistic: either too high or too low.
188   10. Résumés of key personnel were inadequate.
189   11. Personnel lacked experience or the required qualifications.
190   12. The proposal was poorly written and not well organised.
191   13. The proposal did not follow the organisational pattern
192   specified in the RFP.
193   14. The completed proposal was not attractive.
194   15. The proposal did not provide adequate assurance that
195   completion deadlines would be met.
196   16. Essential data were not included in the proposal.
197   17. The proposed facilities were inadequate.
198   18. The proposal failed to show that essential equipment and
199   facilities were available.
200   19. The proposed time schedule was unrealistic.
201   20. The proposal failed to include the qualifications of the
202   submitting organisation.
203   (Bowman and Branchaw, 1992)

204   The above arguments have hopefully proven how important is the
205   role that extralingual factors play. Nonetheless, the above list of
206   possible causes for rejection sheds even more light on this. Just

207 to mention one obvious issue: if the proposal does not arrive by
208 the submission deadline, is this fact related in any way to
209 linguistics? In any event, the deadline is a basic requirement to
210 be fulfilled, which (under given circumstances) becomes an issue
211 of professional ethics.
212   On the other hand, linguistic elements also have an important
213 function to fulfil. If we just consider translations of proposals, they
214 can help to address the right audience, to define the objectives
215 well and to ensure the proposal is well written, well organised and
216 attractive.
217   How do we teach proposal writing? Teaching is similar to most
218 genres in Professional Documentation and to methods proposed
219 by Paltridge (2002). Students need to be exposed to sample
220 proposals as possible models for their writing. Students are asked
221 to identify the typical macro-structure of the given proposal.
222 Together with the instructor, they examine the way the sample text
223 is divided up into sections, as well as consider the function each
224 of these sections performs in achieving its overall goal.

225   **Bibliography**
226 Békési, I., Petőfi, S.J. and Vass, L., Gondolatok a szövegtani
227   kutatás soron következő feladataihoz. A szaknyelvi szövegek
228   szövegtani elemzése felé. In S. János Petőfi, Imre Békési and
229   László Vass (szerk.), *Szemiotikai Szövegtan.* 12. Szövegtani
230   kutatás: témák, eredmények, feladatok. Szeged: JGYTF,
231   pp. 11–16, 1999.

232 Bowman, J.P. and Branchaw, B.P., *How to Write Proposals that*
233   *Produce.* Phoenix, AZ: Oryx Press, 1992.

234 Brockbank, E., The translator is a writer. *Translation Journal,* 5(2),
235   2001. *http://accurapid.com/journal/16prof.htm.*

236 Connor, U. and Mauranen, A., Linguistic analysis of grant
237   proposals: European Union research grants. *English for*
238   *Specific Purposes,* 18(1), pp. 47–62, 1999.

239 Haselkorn, M.P., Proposals. In M.G. Moran and D. Journet (eds),
240   *Research in Technical Communication.* Westport, CT:
241   Greenwood Press, pp. 255–83, 1985.

242 Koltay, T., Including technical and academic writing in translation
243   curricula. *Translation Journal,* 2(2), 1998. *http://accurapid*
244   *.com/journal/04educ.htm.*

245   Paltridge, B., Thesis and dissertation writing: an examination of
246   published advice and actual practice. *English for Specific*
247   *Purposes*, 21(2), pp. 125–43, 2002.

Analysis

The analysed text contains 2,050 words (1,903 without references).

The first 18 lines of the original contain introductory remarks. The very first sentence in line 2 cites the author's own paper, published in the journal, indicating that this paper is the continuation of an earlier one. Some of the earlier arguments are even repeated in a short form. Line 10 reminds the reader of the concept of Professional Documentation (PD). The properly presented abbreviation appears then in the next few sentences. Line 19 contains a reference, thus it is not needed in the abstract.

Line 23 is where important information appears. Up to line 30, the sentences display content that can and should be condensed. We repeat it here together with the condensed version.

> One of the genres such writing education can make use of is the proposal. Proposals represent a genre that is highly useful for any writer, including translators. Well-written proposals multiply the chances of being accepted. In many cases proposals have to be prepared in two or more languages. Translators familiar with the genre and the cultural differences between the source and the target language can render a highly useful service. This is true even if we know that proposals differ by their type and conditions of their submission.

This original can be transformed into the following:

> Proposals are highly useful for any writer, especially translators, as in many cases proposals have to be prepared in two or more languages. Familiarity with the genre and the cultural differences between the source and the target language is highly useful in this.

The sentence in line 31 indicates that the author gives importance to this fact. It states: 'As we will see, proposal writing is strongly related to extralingual information.' The following sentences, nonetheless, contain theoretical considerations related to the linguistic nature of proposals, while the article discusses mainly practical aspects of the genre. Consequently, this idea can be left out of the abstract. A definition of the proposal comes in line 41 that begins with the following words: 'Coming back to proposals, ...' In the original, the function of this phrase is to direct attention to the importance of the subsequent sentences, which begin after a digression.

A shortened version of this definition will be included in the abstract and it is reasonable to put it in at the beginning. From line 44, we find the details that pertain to the definition but do not need to include them in the abstract. With line 54, we find one of the most frequent difficulties of this text: it contains a relatively high number of lists. Such lists have to be transformed into linear text which sometimes can prove difficult. In any case, the last explanation, added to the concept of internal proposals, has to be eliminated, even though it is not self-explanatory that the internal nature of proposals means that writers and readers are members of the same organisation. The sentences between lines 63 and 95 contain information about the audience. Below you can see one of the possible solutions to include this information in the abstract.

To put the ten rhetorical moves, mentioned first in line 99 and enumerated in a bulleted list, properly is a demanding task. Starting with line 96, we offer the following solution:

> A linguistic analysis of research grant proposals identified ten rhetorical moves. Besides the moves, characterising all article introductions, there were moves on the anticipated results, the benefits of the study. The writers claimed competence in carrying out the proposed tasks and underlined its importance.

To be able to do this properly, awareness of the concept of the rhetorical moves, their role in the introductions of scientific articles and familiarity with writing proposals is necessary.

The bulleted list that begins with line 156 contains two different types of description of the problems related to the rejection of proposals. There is a short, keyword-like description and a detailed one.

While using the short descriptions could seem obvious, the negative words do not say much about the problems. It is, consequently, more suitable to combine the two into short phrases, as follows:

> The readers may not trust the writers and they may not see that the problem is sufficiently important or urgent or of high priority. They may not believe that the proposed solution will provide an adequate return on investment.

The last, this time numbered, list that begins on line 177 continues this topic. It enumerates more reasons why proposals are rejected. The 20 items have to be compressed into a shorter unit.

Line 217 contains a question: 'How do you teach proposal writing?' Readers of the abstract are, naturally, interested not in the question but in the answer to it. The problem lies in the proportions of the article. Even if its title suggests that it is about teaching proposal writing, it says much more about the genre itself than about teaching methods.

Draft abstract

A written proposal is a document in which the writer offers something beneficial to the reader in exchange for something in return. Proposals are highly useful for any writer, especially including translators, as in many cases proposals have to be prepared in two or more languages. Familiarity with the genre and the cultural differences between the source and the target language is highly useful in this.

Proposals can be submitted to apply for government, foundation and corporate grants. They may be internal and include bids for government and commercial contracts.

Proposals have to reach their primary, secondary and intermediate audience that may include technical and non-technical readers. It is useful to answer questions related to the real audience, its existing knowledge, interests and perception. A linguistic analysis of research grant proposals identified ten rhetorical moves. Besides these moves characterising all article introductions, there were moves on the anticipated results and the benefits of the study. The writers claimed competence in carrying out the proposed tasks and underlined its importance.

The rejection of proposals can have different causes. The readers may not trust the writers and they may not see that the problem is sufficiently important or urgent or of high priority. They may not believe that the proposed solution will provide an adequate return on investment. The reasons for rejection may include not observing the submission deadline, failing to demonstrate a clear understanding of the problem or failing to define the objectives properly. The proposers might address the wrong audience. The proposal may fail to show that essential equipment and facilities are available and that the experience and qualifications of key personnel are adequate. The proposed time schedule may be unrealistic. The overall design may be questionable or cost estimates not realistic. The proposal may be poorly written or is not otherwise attractive.

Students need to be exposed to sample proposals as possible models for their writing. They identify the typical macro-structures of the proposals and the division of sample texts.

Comments

The draft abstract contains 348 words. Its size is not too far from the ideal if we regard the 250-word limit as standard. There is, nonetheless, need for general revision and a higher degree of brevity can be achieved.

The edited version

The proposal is a document in which the writer offers something beneficial to the reader in exchange for something in return. Besides general writers, familiarity with proposals is useful for translators, as in many cases proposals have to be prepared in two or more languages. Proposals can be submitted to apply for government, foundation and corporate grants. They may be internal and include bids for government and commercial contracts. Good proposals have to reach their primary, secondary and intermediate audience that may include technical and non-technical readers.

Besides the rhetorical moves characterising all article introductions, research grant proposals contain moves on the anticipated results, the benefits of the study and competence in carrying out the proposed tasks.

Proposals may be rejected because of the lack of trust in the writers, or because the writer could not demonstrate the importance, urgency or high priority of the problem. Not observing the submission deadline, addressing the wrong audience or not demonstrating a clear understanding of the problem are sources of rejection. Failing to demonstrate the objectives properly or not showing that essential equipment and facilities are available also can cause rejection, as well as the unsatisfactory demonstration of required experience and qualifications of key personnel. Proposals may be rejected because of unrealistic and questionable overall design, unrealistic time schedule or cost estimates. Rejected proposals may be poorly written or unattractive.

Students need to be exposed to sample proposals and made to identify the typical macro-structures of the proposals and the division of sample texts.

Comments on the edited version

The final version is 251 words long. At this size, it is just above the 250-word limit. Some of the details of the editing process teach us the following lessons.

The attribute 'written' is not of vital importance in the definition, so it can be erased from the first sentence. The second sentence had to be edited rather substantially. Taken from line 80, the word 'good' was added to the sentence that speaks about the audience in order to show that we are discussing ideal proposals. The sentence 'It is useful to answer questions, related to the real audience, its existing knowledge, interests and perception' provides a minimum of new information so can be deleted.

The sentence 'A linguistic analysis of research grant proposals identified ten rhetorical moves' is superfluous. The identification of research grant proposals is, nonetheless, useful. The sentence 'Familiarity with the genre and the cultural differences between the source and the target language is highly useful in this' can be eliminated, as there is no concrete discussion of these differences.

Beyond language and style

This chapter could also be called 'Beyond practical questions and elementary theory of abstracting'. In it, we intend to give a more detailed treatment of issues which were partially touched upon in the previous parts of the book. They will be of continuing interest for those who want to be acquainted with these problems beyond the strictly practical issues of abstracting. While this chapter may not definitely be considered 'obligatory' reading in this book, we are convinced, nonetheless, that it addresses questions that are of the utmost interest and deserve the attention of the reader.

Our argument below takes into consideration that abstracts and abstracting are constrained by the following complexities:

- Abstracts and abstracting constitute a system – abstracts are physical containers of reduced information.
- Abstracts exist in information and communication.
- Abstracts result in information processes. (Pinto, 2003b)

The chapter consists of two parts which could be classified as distinct essays. The first is a complex discussion of several issues. It continues to present knowledge on the abstracting process, thus completing the picture the elements of which have appeared throughout this book. The analysis is continued by providing some models of the process and giving details that pertain to a number of other related processes. We also examine the abstract as a genre in its own right. The second part is equally complex, although not by virtue of the multitude of topics. It addresses the elaborate relationship between abstracting and text comprehension.

Approaches and models

It may seem obvious, but to be able to produce better quality abstracts it is better to know as much as possible about the abstracting process (Tibbo, 1992; Pinto, 2006). Despite extensive discussion of the different aspects of the abstracting process in the previous chapters, there are still issues to be examined and presented to the interested reader. This knowledge is very much related to the question of how we can approach abstracting. Approaches that are based on thorough methodologies frequently result in models, and being acquainted with models is in general beneficial. We hope also that the models we wish to present will prove beneficial as well.

We can look at abstracting as an activity that can be broken down into a number of different steps. From this point of view, any activity, including communicative acts, consists of three main phases:

- engaging with information (reading);
- extracting information;
- presenting information. (Eisenberg, 2007)

Analysis and synthesis – or, as Sparck Jones (1993) names these processes, forming a representation of the original and synthesis of the summary – are influenced by the following aspects found in the originals:

- statement of the problem that the authors are addressing: why are they writing?

- the potential audience;

- the solution (a thesis, if there is one) to the problem that the authors suggest;

- the methods of argumentation that the authors use;

- the types of evidence they present;

- the conclusions they reach. (Manion, 2008)

Abstracting is influenced by a number of variables on different levels. Pinto and Gálvez (1999) distinguish five such variables:

1. The original.

2. The recipient.

3. Media:

    – the source storage media;

    – the source transmission media;

    – the recipient's reception media;

    – the recipient's storage media.

4. The social context of information transfer:

    – the need for information;

    – the information distribution channels;

    – the effects on the audience;

    – national and foreign information policies.

5. Quality:

    – the quality of information selection;

    – the quality of information presentation;

    – the quality of information impact.

We know that originals are scientific papers published in scholarly journals. As regards the recipients, we need to add that the specific social context in which relations among sources, recipients and channels take place must also be stressed. To analyse the different audiences' needs and their effects on abstracts acquires especial importance. Similarly, the recipients' (users') cognitive state, with regard to their information requirements and needs, is significant (Pinto and Gálvez, 1999). Overall, we have a relatively clear-cut picture of the recipients of abstracts.

All these variables would look as follows:

Originals	Scientific papers
Recipients	Researchers and practitioners
Media	Written text, fixed on paper or other (electronic, optical) storage media
The social context	Express need for information Formal channels of distribution
Quality	Need for high quality (in all aspects)

All or some of these variables can appear in the different models of abstracting. In the literature, we can find a substantial number of graphic models that represent abstracting or some of the processes related to abstracting, and such models are offered by, among others, Lancaster (1991), Pinto (1995) and Endres-Niggemeyer (1998). Nevertheless, there are yet more worthwhile models to consider.

One of these is a simple, linear model of translation. It is applicable to our case, because abstracting and translation show a number of similarities. Both are processes of linguistic mediation. As described by Bańczerowski (2000c), its participants are the following:

sender → text A → translator → text B → recipient

The phases of translation are as follows:

> original text → reception → identification → decoding → translation → coding → mediation → terminal text

Translators, in a similar way to language teachers and language learners, are both senders and recipients (Bańczerowski, 2000c). This is true also for abstracting. Consequently, the elements of the above model can serve as components in a model of abstracting. Taking into consideration that both the translator and the abstractor fulfil the dual roles of sender and recipient, we can substitute the translator for the abstractor.

> sender → text A → *abstractor* → text B → recipient

The phases of *abstracting* are as follows:

> original text → reception → identification → decoding → summarising → coding → mediation → terminal text (*abstract*)

If we consider this model, we can agree with Werlich (1988) who states that in abstracting the original text is translated into a new text.

All above similarities with translation come from the predominantly linguistic nature of the operations that comprise both activities. In addition to this, both abstracting and translation are communication processes that require the presence of a mediating person, who is required to have linguistic skills and professional knowledge. As mentioned in Chapter 4, this professional is not involved in these activities accidentally. In particular abstracting is an activity which requires some kind of commissioning, usually in the form of an order from an abstracting service. Practically no one writes abstracts on their own initiative or for the sake of their own entertainment, while translation can take place as a result of personal motivation or for private goals.

In this case and in similar situations the translation of the whole text is often not required, but a kind of summary is (or would be) needed which conveys the essence of the text in the unknown language. This also shows the closeness of the relationship between abstracting and translation (Hutchins, 1993).

There are, evidently, differences between translation and abstracting. In the case of translation we always name the source and target languages. The original text is in a source language, while the terminal text is in a target language which is different from the source language. The translation processes are different from those of abstracting and the phases that bear the same name cover different processes. Mediation is also different. In spite of this, abstracting can be both inter-lingual and intra-lingual. Intra-lingual means that the original text and the abstract are in the same language while in the case of inter-lingual abstracting the original and the abstract are in two different languages. In such cases, there is a complex relationship between competencies in the native and in the foreign language. Inter-lingual abstracting presupposes not only that we understand discourse perfectly, but requires experience in this cognitive performance in the mother tongue (Gläser, 1993; Uso and Palmer, 1998). In other words, insufficient awareness and knowledge of the linguistic and rhetorical structures of abstracts in the source language and in the target language can cause numerous problems in this context (Busch-Lauer, 1995).

There is a more profound conceptual difference, as well. Translation is supposed to be equivalent to the original.

While there is not the space here to analyse and evaluate in detail one of the most problematic and controversial areas in the field of translation theory that has caused heated debates (Leonardi, 2000), we can state that there has to be equivalence between the source language text and the target language text. This can appear:

- on the referential level, as both texts are related to the same reality;

- on the functional level, as both texts fulfil the same communicative role;

- on the contextual level, as the sentences of the target language have to fulfil the same function as the sentences in the source text. (Klaudy, 1979)

Abstracts are different. On the referential level, they are equivalent to the original text, as both are based on and are related to the same reality. Despite this, differences appear already at the functional level, as the communicative roles of the original and of the abstract are different. We can state this without any further explanation, as our arguments set forth in earlier parts of this book have verified this sufficiently. The situation is similar at the contextual level, as there can be little argument that the sentences of the original (the target language text) and those of the abstract (the source language text) fulfil different functions.

Instead of striving for equivalence, abstracting produces a deliberately *heterovalent* target text, the abstract. The main cause of this lies in the fact that the abstract is dependent on the original only at the content level. Primarily, this means that the original's style and the order of explanation do not have a direct influence on the text of the abstract (Pfeiffer-Jäger, 1980). It is not a coincidence that Collison (1971) directs our attention to the fact that abstracting from a

181

foreign language requires paraphrasing and interpretation to a greater extent compared to intra-lingual abstracting. It shows the hetarovalent nature of transformations.

There is heterovalence in the content, as well. Equivalence would not be possible, because one of the main operations of abstracting is the omission of elements of the original's content that are judged to be of lesser importance. We know how central the question of importance of information is. This becomes visible in the abstracting process. As a result of reading the original, the semantic structure of the original text becomes clear, thus we obtain the explicit content of the original. Further analysis results in the selection of the more important and deselection of the less important content (Karasev, 1978). In general terms, selection is a process of purposeful elimination through contraction, reduction and condensation (Pinto et al., 2008). It is also a process of generalising from the particular and identifying the general (global) structure (Hutchins, 1993).

These activities require the abstractor to possess world knowledge and they are influenced by the level of information needs and by the requirements that are set by the given abstracting service. All these processes are influenced by the level of knowledge in the given field, the level of needs defined by the target audience and the requirements set up by the abstracting service (Karasev, 1978). If nothing else, this deeply influences the resulting heterovalence.

Be that as it may, there is a type of 'translation' that is worth mentioning here. Although of a distinctive quality, subject indexing is mediation. It is not by chance that abstracting and indexing are usually treated as closely interrelated problems. The reason for this is that the main purpose of both abstracting and indexing is to construct representations of published items in a form suitable for inclusion in some type of database (Lancaster, 1991).

Abstracting and indexing can be placed in the category of Written Text Documentary Content Analysis (WTDCA), which is content analysis restricted to the limits of written textual documents and documentary (informational) goals. WTDCA consists of the examination of written texts in order to determine their content followed by some kind of description. The main activities of WTDCA are indexing and abstracting. Methodologies for WTDCA come from a number of disciplines such as textual linguistics, formal logic and cognitive psychology. The documentary nature of content analysis means that it is 'endowed with the appropriate informative capacity in accordance with the previously established demands of the user' (Pinto, 1994: 132). While on the subject of content analysis, it is worth mentioning that it is not enough to approach content as something describable by the number of words and other 'observable' features. We have to examine its complex dimensions instead (Van Dijk, 1996).

Knowledge on indexing can be found in a number of textbooks (Cleveland and Cleveland, 1983; Lancaster, 1991; Rowley, 1988) and it is beyond the scope of this book to provide a substantial treatment of indexing. Nevertheless, indexing and abstracting coincide in their need of an analytical stage which is partially the same in both. The difference arises in synthesis, as indexing results in sets of words while abstracts convey a message in the form of cohesive and coherent verbal texts (Pinto, 1995).

If we approach abstracting as a process of communication, the model devised by Sidorov (1982) can be of good use. This is a relatively complex model of an extended communication. To be able to model abstracting, we need a general model of communication which includes the following subsystems, as illustrated in Figure 7.1:

Figure 7.1 A communicative model of abstracting

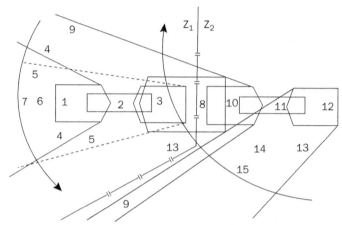

Source: Sidorov (1982). Used by permission.

1. Activities of the sender.
2. The original text.
3. Activities of the recipient.
4. Knowledge and skills of the sender.
5. Knowledge and skills of the recipient.
6. Conceptual space of the communication.
7. Factual space of the communication.

Abstracting communication is characterised by the fact that the abstractor is inserted into this communicational chain. Thus the following subsystems also have to be added to the model:

8. The receptive phase of abstracting.
9. Knowledge and skills of the abstractor.
10. The productive phase of abstracting.
11. The text of the abstract.
12. Activities of the recipient of the abstract.

13. Knowledge and skills of the recipient of the abstract.

14. Conceptual space of the abstracting communication.

15. Factual space of the abstracting communication.

In analysing this figure we want to concentrate on a selected set of phenomena and circumstances, as follows.

The psychical acquisition of the factual space of the communication (7) goes through here. The limits of this are defined by the contiguity of the knowledge and skills of the sender (4) and those of the recipient (5), which comprise the conceptual space of the communication (6). This determines the communicative activities of the sender (1).

Activities of the sender accommodate an ideal picture about the activities of the recipient (3). The activities of the sender are directed towards the original text (2), which is generated as a result of the activities of the sender (1) with the aim of enabling the activities of the recipient (3) and making them successful.

The activities of the recipient are covered by the activities of the sender in the form of an ideal conception and a flexible programme of generating the text. The factual space of the communication (7) goes together with its conceptual space (6). They pertain to the activities of the sender. The original text is an integral part of the activities of the recipient and these are the activities which are instrumental in reconstructing the activities of the sender. As the activities of the sender accommodate an ideal picture of the activities of the recipient, this ideal picture materialises as a text that functions within the framework of the activities of the sender. In the receptive phase of abstracting (8) reception of the original text is only one of the activities of the abstractor and it is similar to the activities of the sender. Communicative activities of the abstractor, however, do not end here. While the activities of the sender (3) represent full-value activities, the receptive phase of abstracting is only one, albeit indispensable, step in a complex of activities.

The receptive phase of abstracting is extraneous from the viewpoint of the text and does not influence its communicative structure. The receptive phase is based not on the original text but on the ideal picture of the abstract production and on the activities of the recipient.

The receptive and the productive phases of abstracting (8) (10) are the communicative activities of the abstractor. In these activities the original text, which is the object of the abstractor's activities, is incorporated. This text, nonetheless, does not postulate the existence of the abstractor, because the aim of the abstractor's communicative activities is to produce the text of the abstract (11).

There is a mutual determination between the receptive phase of abstracting, its productive phase and the text of the abstract. The latter is one of the main carriers of determination and its functioning is based on the receptive and productive phases. These phases materialise in the text of the abstract which, on the other hand, influences these subsystems.

The activities of the abstractor do not influence the original text, which is the result of the primary communication (2), as it comes into existence without postulating these activities.

Z_1 designates the source language and Z_2 the target language. They may be identical. If not, translation goes in parallel with summarisation and is carried out in the receptive phase of abstracting (Sidorov, 1982). The model in Figure 7.1 supports the idea that it is essential to be able to explain not only how information is comprehended, but also how it is represented and synthesised (Pinto and Gálvez, 1999). Problems of presentation arise because there are a number of demands set against the resulting text: it has to be an abstract as we defined it and as the needs of the recipients, mediated by the abstracting service, determine it.

The subtitle of this book is 'A genre and set of skills for the twenty-first century'. It should consequently address the issue of genres. Among the genres of scientific and technical communication, the abstract constitutes a genre in its own right (Lorés 2004). This is the reason why the success of author abstracts 'largely depends on both linguistic competence and knowledge of the appropriate structure of genres and the forms of their linguistic representation' (Busch-Lauer, 1995: 769).

It is not the aim of this chapter to give a comprehensive treatment of the issue of the genre. We simply repeat the words of Rosso (2008: 20) instead:

> Genre names are useful for referring to communication in the recurring situations in which we find ourselves – whether it's looking for a job/hiring someone (a résumé) or acknowledging a thoughtful gift/having that gift acknowledged (a thank-you letter).

It is helpful, nonetheless, to consider the concept of the genre in greater detail. First of all, we should note that library and information science is interested in genre theory. As Andersen (2008: 31) puts it:

> As LIS is interested in how knowledge in documents and other artefacts is organized, genre theory is a productive perspective. Studying genres reveals that genres and human activity are important organizing factors of communication and knowledge. It tells us what kinds of genres various people and institutions in various communicative contexts prefer. A genre view of these communicative activities provides a means to

systemically examine document production and use and the organization of document production and use.

We can define genre as 'a prototypical class of texts, a historically established, institutionalized and productive pattern for the logical ordering (disposition, elaboration) and the linguistic formulation of a subject-specific matter or state of affairs' (Gläser, 1993).

Genres are also socially recognised ways of using language accepted by the members of a given community, as it answers their expectations (Hyland, 2007). Genre studies are concerned not only with text types, but with different typified human activities that are related to the use of texts. In studying genre, we focus on people and the production and use of various documents. Yet, besides production and use we should also view how documents help people to do their work (Andersen, 2008). Knowledge of genre is also an individual's repertoire that is formed to give appropriate responses to recurrent situations (Berkenkotter and Huckin, 1995).

Professional language and literature, showing a distinct style, a characteristic choice of terms, etc., play a key role in establishing the cultural identity of a disciplinary community. Many elements of this language originate in the community's traditions, customs, practices, beliefs and morals, as well as symbolic forms of communication (Elmborg, 2006). Academic genres derive from the individuals' participation in the communicative activities of daily and professional life and genres are owned by the given community (Berkenkotter and Huckin, 1995).

Without academic genres, it would be impossible to engage in scholarship. Elmborg (2006: 197) expresses this as follows:

> Genres provide us with explicit patterns for creating academic work – the ways we construct our identities

as writers and researchers, the ways we construct and interpret our major statements and use evidence, and the ways we conceive of the communities we address with our scholarship.

In the light of all these, it is clear why articles present the processes and results of investigations in a form that might be accepted by fellow colleagues in the given field (Trawinski, 1989).

Swales (1990: 58) states that 'a genre is a class of communicative events, the members of which share some set of communicative purposes'. This communicative function of the genre is what 'shapes structure, style, content and intended audience' (Cross and Oppenheim, 2006: 435). This theory is based on the assumption that writers first acquire explicit knowledge of a particular form of writing. This is followed by getting acquainted with specific structures, identifying the specific information elements (content) required by the given genre and following the specific language rules that have to be applied consistently. These conventions (often called rhetoric) feature a particular genre (Chan and Foo, 2001).

Both form and content are essential constituents of genre knowledge. One crucial aspect of genre is background knowledge that the readers of the given genre are assumed to have (Berkenkotter and Huckin, 1995).

A good way to find some distinctive features of the genre 'abstract' is to compare it with article introductions. Although it is clear that abstracts should not be confused with introductions the relationship between them is quite complex (Hughes, 2006; Samraj, 2005).

Author abstracts are usually placed after the title of the article and the affiliation of the author(s). They precede the main text, thus they are placed next and closest to introductions that are part of the original's main text, as explained in Chapter 5. There seems to be general agreement that abstracts differ from original texts in their function, their rhetorical structure and their linguistic realisations (Lorés, 2004). These three areas are closely connected to each other, as the functions of the given abstract determine both its global structure and its linguistic realisation.

The function of introductions is to present the research problem and objectives, as well as review existing literature on the subject. Abstracts, in contrast, reflect the content of the whole article, albeit selectively. Information contained in the introductions of original texts is thus treated selectively because background information and the literature review, which are undoubtedly located in the introduction, have no place in abstracts.

The rhetorical structure of abstracts is usually defined by the structure of the original. This structure is apparently flexible. Introductions, in contrast, have a well-known formula that makes their writing relatively simple, which is true especially in the case of papers in the natural sciences. The CARS (Create a Research Space) model, for example, is a characteristic feature of article introductions. It consists of three phases, each made up of different steps:

- establishing a territory;
- establishing a niche;
- occupying this niche. (Swales, 1990)

As regards the length, introductions should be short but do not have a word limit as abstracts do. Their main purpose is to introduce the research by presenting its context or background. Introductions usually go from the general to the specific, introducing the research problem and the ways of investigating it. As mentioned before, this is very much a widespread general structure of papers.

Different sections of journal articles differ from each other in their readability. Measures made of the overall readability of various types of text, as well as of sentence lengths, difficult and unique words, articles, prepositions and pronouns, showed that abstracts scored worst on most of these measures. Introductions came next (Hartley et al., 2003). As we stressed in the subsection on evaluation in Chapter 5, measuring the readability of abstracts does not seem to make a significant contribution to their evaluation.

One of the main features of abstracts that distinguishes them from other genres is that they centre on the appreciation of novelty and thus help to screen original and novel contributions to an academic discipline (Berkenkotter and Huckin, 1995).

Objectivity, depicted in Chapter 3, also distinguishes this genre. As Werlich (1988) states, abstracts are expository texts that contain analyses of relatively complex matters that are then explained in an objective and precise way. Abstracting is determined by a convergence between objective and subjective reality. The former is present foremost in the original. The carrier of subjective reality is the abstractor, who shows different levels of knowledge and personal, non-transferable targets (Pinto et al., 2008a). Subjective reality has clear-cut boundaries, because the content of abstracts should not go beyond that of the original.

Objective reality has its constraints in the sense that the original text is only one possible representation of it. It has its individual authors, who reflect on reality through their knowledge and beliefs, even if they seriously observe the rules of scientific inquiry. Abstractors have the task of finding and representing important elements of the original text that are worthy of attention. With this, they put the content of the original somewhat closer to objective reality.

Abstracting and comprehension

Abstracting goes beyond simple forms of communication. It is embedded in the processes of selection and structuring of information and it would be unimaginable without deep understanding (comprehension) of the original text (Sherrard, 1985; Pinto et al., 2008a).

One of the major limitations of comprehension is, however, that the capacity of our working memory is limited. Nevertheless, there is a key to this problem. To enable comprehension, we store shortened representations in our memory (Endres-Niggemeyer, 1998; Pinto, 2006a).

The connection between abstracting and comprehension is based on the fact that the act of determining what is important also plays a decisive role in general comprehension (Asaf and Garza, 2007).

It is reasonable to assume that abstractors comprehend the text in the same way as fluent readers. There are, nevertheless, significant differences. Abstractors work under time constraints, comprehend the text solely for the purpose of abstracting, the comprehension is directly followed by text production, and much of the work lies within a narrow range of text types and subject fields (Farrow, 1991).

Comprehension is a complex process which uses existing knowledge to make sense of new information. We ask questions about the text before, during and after reading, we draw inferences from the text and we monitor our own comprehension. Comprehension would be impossible without the integration of the information contained in the textual object into the knowledge of the reader in a coherent form. To reach better understanding, the reader has to move constantly between deep and surface structures of the text. The latter presupposes the knowledge of the lexicon, that is the reader has to understand the words used in the given text. Comprehension also requires syntactical (grammatical) knowledge. To be able to comprehend the deep structures of the text, there is a need to have general background knowledge (or world knowledge, in other words), as well as knowledge about the topic of the given text. The more knowledge the reader has, the better are the chances that the comprehension will be optimal. Different levels of knowledge produce different results in comprehension of the same text (Pinto et al., 2005). Knowledge of text typologies is also needed (Endres-Niggemeyer, 1998). These principles support the criteria of the abstractors' knowledge base that we outlined in Chapter 4.

The concepts of the 'deep structure' and 'surface structure' have been established by representatives of transformational grammar (transformational-generative grammar), especially by the American linguist Noam Chomsky. Transformational grammar tries to show that in their underlying structure – that is in their deeper relations to one another – sentences are very similar. Although defined differently by each linguist, surface structures are the actual words and sounds used, while deep structures carry a sentence's underlying meaning ('Deep structure', 2009).

A proposition is that part of the meaning of a clause or sentence that is constant (SIL International, 2004). This requires that we hold only high-level shortened, compressed representations of the discourse in question in our memory. It is much easier to manage and to keep them in memory than large sequences of complex semantic structures (Van Dijk, 1980). This is the solution to storage of meaning within the limited capacity of our working memory.

Abstracting is a complex chain of operations that implies the transformation of textual documents from their surface and rhetorical structures towards their deep (content) structure by generating shortened representations of texts

(Pinto, 1995). Discourse comprehension is the prologue and epilogue to summarisation and – in particular – to abstracting. Summarisation processes and techniques are closely related to the cognitive processes of abstracting, as we understand text by summarisation, the essence of which is controlled forgetting (Endres-Niggemeyer, 1998).

Differentiating between deep and surface structures is basically identical to differentiating between local and global structures of discourse. Global structures represent the content of the discourse – in other words, what is considered relevant, central or crucial to what is being communicated. These global structures are called *macrostructures. Microstructures*, in contrast, represent the style of expression. Macrostructures enable the reduction of complex information to information that is more relevant, abstract or general (Van Dijk, 1980).

The main idea behind the concept of the macrostructure is the hypothesis that it is possible to establish a homology between the deep structure of a sentence and that of a text. The macrostructure of the text corresponds to the structural coherence of a sentence (Rulewicz, 1995). When we apply macrostructures, it is not only easier to recall global meanings, but macrostructures also explain how and why language users are able to summarise texts (Van Dijk, 2005).

Macro-level analysis serves an overall understanding of the 'aboutness' and meaning of the complete text as a whole (Beghtol, 1986).

In connection with macrostructures, Kintsch and Van Dijk (1983) developed a model for the cognitive representation of text which assumes that similar structures are assigned to a discourse in the cases of production, comprehension and other processes including summarisation. This model is particularly useful in understanding the processes of abstracting (Cross and Oppenheim, 2006).

Summarisation represents an attempt to establish (or reconstruct) the macrostructure of the discourse. At a certain point in the process of comprehension, the representations that result from summarisation can be identical to informative abstracts. Further compression of information can result in indicative abstracts (Endres-Niggemeyer, 1998). The similarity between the original and the text of the informative abstract can be compared to the similarity between two triangles that have the same angles but the sides are different as in all levels of discourse general and specific components conserve the 'shape' of information (Manning, 1990).

As a summary is the expression of the macrostructure of a text, it is interpreted by individuals in the light of their background knowledge. In consequence, there can be different summaries for the same text (Hutchins, 1987).

In theoretical terms, summarisation involves four components:

- the comprehension of a given microstructure;
- the identification of global schemata (superstructures);
- the application of macro-rules (macro-strategies);
- the expression of the macrostructure as a coherent text (Hutchins, 1987).

We will discuss all these below.

In the case of abstracting macro-strategies serve as goal-setting strategies and are concerned essentially with the identification of important propositions (Endres-Niggemeyer, 1998).

Comprehension involves both top-down and bottom-up processing. Top-down processing uses information that is not contained in the text but is part of the world-knowledge that the author possesses and which is assumed that the readers will also possess. This is extra-linguistic, conventional knowledge of the world and knowledge of the subject matter of the text (Beghtol, 1986; Farrow, 1991). This knowledge plays a role in formulating and testing hypotheses regarding both the 'aboutness' and the meaning of the text (Beghtol, 1986). As we have already pointed out, finding out what documents are about is one of the main concerns of information professionals (Hutchins, 1977). Searching for 'aboutness' and meaning are related to these efforts. They are nonetheless extremely complex and their treatment is often controversial. It is consequently beyond the scope of this book to give any comprehensive analysis of these issues.

In executing bottom-up (conceptual) processing, readers perform an analysis of the microstructure. As Beghtol (1986: 86) points it out, during the reading process 'the reader notices the presentation of each sentence, automatically transforms its surface verbal structures into its deep conceptual propositions and establishes an understanding of the logical relationships between the words and sentences of the text'.

Besides macrostructures and microstructures, we may distinguish a third category, *superstructures*. They are not identical with macrostructures. Superstructures are global structures, not of meaning but of form. Superstructures reflect the organisation of macro-propositions of discourse in conventional formats like the scientific article (Van Dijk, 2005). Superstructures are not superordinate structures. They may be considered much more a transition between surface and deep structures (Pinto, 1992). Superstructures have a significant practical use. They provide invaluable help in identifying important information to be abstracted, even though they are not identical with it. Superstructures are marked, among other ways, by the headings and subheadings of the article, e.g. 'Introduction' or 'Discussion'.

Macrostructures are derived from microstructures by the operations of four types of macro-strategies, which are purpose-oriented processes of information reduction (Van Dijk, 1980). There are four macro-strategies. We present them below, based on the works of Kintsch and Van Dijk (1983), Hutchins (1983) and Sherrard (1985).

- *Deletion* operates negatively by eliminating unnecessary and irrelevant information, such as detailed descriptions, background information or common knowledge. An example of applying the *deletion* rule is the following set of sentences: *We went to the bookstore. It was at the corner. We bought a dictionary.* After deletion: *We went to the bookstore. We bought a dictionary.* The fact that the bookstore is located on the corner is of secondary importance to the message. Another example is: *Mary played with a ball. The ball was blue.* After deletion we have: *Mary played with a ball.*

- *Selection* operates positively by extracting and retaining what is necessary and relevant. Of relevance can be, for example, propositions that express pre-conditions and data essential for the interpretation of other propositions.

- *Generalisation* results in general propositions taken from the semantic detail given in propositions. In other words, a sequence of micro-propositions is replaced by a single micro-proposition. An example of generalisation is the following: *Father was washing dishes. Mother was working on her new book. The daughter was busy painting the window frames.* After generalisation we have: *The whole family was busy.* A further example is: *Mary played with a doll. Mary played with blocks.* After generalisation we have: *Mary played with toys.*

- *Construction* replaces sequences of propositions by single propositions expressing self-contained events or processes. A sequence of propositions can be replaced by a proposition that is entailed by the joint set of propositions of the sequence. An example of construction is as follows: *John went to the station. He bought a ticket. Then he took the train to London. At London Paddington he left it.* After construction we have: *John took the train to London Paddington.*

(Kintsch and Van Dijk, 1983; Hutchins, 1983; Sherrard, 1985)

8

Conclusion

As said earlier in this book, abstracting is a series of small challenges that have to be faced no matter what. The challenges remain with us, despite the changing role that abstracts fulfil. From print indexes, then human-readable outputs of electronic databases, they have developed into computer-searchable surrogates of a substantial body of literature.

Abstracting has not lost its importance: it has a future. This is especially true in the case of author abstracts. In fact, there have never been predictions that they would eventually disappear. Abstracts written by professional abstractors – mainly information professionals who work under different names and have different duties – may well experience changes, but in their role of helping to assess the relevance of documents they continue to be indispensable. Indeed, their importance seems to be growing under the circumstances of the information society with its tremendous flow of freely and easily but uncontrollably available information. This is the point where information literacy comes into play. When we write abstracts, we have to concentrate on deciding what is important in a text. The skills and abilities related to this – in other words attention to the importance of information, one of the main constituents of information literacy – are becoming more and more essential in our whole life, especially in learning environments and in particular in higher education. This attitude stands also at the centre of abstracting.

Abstracts come into being through the process of summarisation. Summarisation may occasionally take on an everyday or semi-professional character. Abstracting, however, is professional summarisation, even though this is not fully recognised by all its stakeholders in scholarly publishing and information production. Despite this we have stressed the professional nature of abstracting and provided a deeper insight into the nature of abstracting, including the relationship between text comprehension and summarisation.

This is the background behind the approaches adopted in this book to present the most important and up-to-date theory of abstracting, as well as advice on and examples of the practice of writing different kinds of abstracts.

Our readers, if they have followed our suggestions about how to read this book or have simply read it as they deemed appropriate, are now hopefully convinced that all this complex of issues is worth their attention.

Our readers, who are most probably professional abstractors (usually information professionals), as well as researchers publishing articles in scholarly journals, linguists and language teachers, will have found in this book a comprehensive coverage and synthesis of a diverse body of knowledge on abstracts and abstracting. They should also be able to identify new points of view in a field which is plagued by often misleading terminology and widespread flawed beliefs. In this regard informative abstracts, widely treated with distinction by virtue of their outstanding role, have received a novel and complex treatment, without losing sight of a host of relevant and important issues.

While not wanting to draw up a full list of the questions addressed in this book, we do want to remind the reader of those that have received treatment, such as the problem of the usefulness of abstracts or the limited possibility of producing abstracts by computers.

Linguists, especially those interested in English for Specific Purposes (ESP) and English for Academic Purposes (EAP), as well as English as a Second Language (ESL) or English as a Foreign Language (EFL) and technical writing, may be interested to find out more about this genre and the related processes and skills. The book serves them, among others, by helping to identify interdisciplinary and cross-disciplinary issues and approaches, many of which may go beyond their interest. Nonetheless, investigating these will prove useful.

To acquire a clear picture about abstracts and abstracting we attempted to remove the ambiguity surrounding the term 'abstract' and related concepts such as the summary, the annotation and the executive summary.

Besides giving a careful treatment to informative abstracts, we also described the nature of indicative and indicative-informative abstracts.

We know that different abstracts fulfil different functions and that from the same source different abstracts can be produced, depending on the goals set for the abstracts, the personality of the abstractor and the point in time of writing the abstract. Similarly, the type and the function of an abstract are closely related.

Abstracts usually aim to provide an objective treatment of information, though there are different levels of objectivity and despite the possibility and partial acceptance of critical abstracts.

The importance of author abstracts and the problems related to them account for the detailed treatment of this sub-genre.

Independently of their other roles, those who are engaged in writing abstracts are required to possess a solid knowledge base consisting of linguistic and extra-linguistic knowledge and to show self-regulation. Reading proficiency and the acquisition of special techniques are indispensable for this.

Half way between theory and practice, a detailed description of the general structure of abstracts, a consideration of the information compulsorily left out of and advisably included in an abstract, the recommended language to use and other aspects were intended to furnish the reader with useful advice, as were a number of abstracting rules.

In addition to the theoretical knowledge imparted in this book, the practical examples represent a modest contribution to help the reader to achieve a professional level in abstracting.

We expect this book will be useful for the education of information professionals both in formal terms and in continuing professional development. Other readers of this book will most probably find use for it in their independent learning and research.

We have defined abstracting as an activity which represents the most important information in a text that is shorter than the original and from a pre-defined viewpoint. Abstracts are thus natural language texts that exist either in written form or fixed on non-paper media. *Mutatis mutandis*, what can be said about this book is that it is the whole world of abstracting in miniature, reflecting this world like an informative abstract reflects the original article. On the other hand, perhaps it is like an indicative-informative abstract – most of its content is explicit enough to be made good use of while minor issues are treated more superficially to prevent the whole burden being loaded onto the shoulders of the reader. Whichever is the case, this book has provided an approach to a genre and set of skills for the twenty-first century.

References

AACU (2002) *Greater Expectations: A New Vision for Learning as a Nation Goes to College.* Washington, DC: Association of American Colleges and Universities.

ACRL (2000) *Information Literacy Competency Standards for Higher Education.* Chicago: Association of College and Research Libraries. Accessed 17 August 2008 online at: *http://www.ala.org/ala/mgrps/divs/acrl/standards/standards.pdf.*

Ad Hoc Working Group for Critical Appraisal of the Medical Literature (1987) 'A proposal for more informative abstracts of clinical articles', *Annals of Internal Medicine*, 106(4): 598–604.

Allen, M. (2008) 'Web 2.0: an argument against convergence', *First Monday*, 13(3). Accessed on 14 March 2008 online at: *http://www.uic.edu/htbin/cgiwrap/bin/ojs/index.php/fm/article/viewArticle/2139/1946.*

American Library Association (ALA) (1989). *American Library Association Presidential Commission on Information Literacy. Final Report.* Chicago: American Library Association.

'Analysis' (2009) See *Wikipedia.* Accessed on 16 June 2009 online at: *http://en.wikipedia.org/wiki/Analysis.*

Andersen, J. (2006) 'The public sphere and discursive activities: information literacy as sociopolitical skills', *Journal of Documentation*, 62(2): 213–28.

Andersen, J. (2008) 'LIS and genre: between people, texts, activity and situation', *Bulletin of the American Society for Information Science and Technology*, 34(5): 31–4. Accessed on 17 August 2008 online at: *http://www.asis .org/Bulletin/Jun-08/JunJul08_Andersen.pdf.*

Anderson, J.D. and Pérez-Carballo, J. (2001) 'The nature of indexing: how humans and machines analyze messages and texts for retrieval. Part I: Research, and the nature of human indexing', *Information Processing and Management*, 37(2): 231–54.

Andretta, S. (2005) *Information Literacy: A Practitioner's Guide*. Oxford: Chandos.

ANSI (1979) *American National Standard for Writing Abstracts*, Z 39.14-1979. American National Standards Institute.

ANSI (1997) *Guidelines for Abstracts*, ANSI/NISO 239.14-1997, Revision of ANSI 239.14-1979 (R1987). Bethesda, MD: NISO Press.

Armstrong, C.J. and Wheatley, A. (1998) 'Writing abstracts for online databases: results of an investigation of database producers' guidelines', *Program*, 32(4): 359–71.

Asaf, L. and Garza, R. (2007) 'Making magazine covers that visually count: learning to summarize with technology', *Reading Teacher*, 60(7): 678–80.

Ashworth, W. (1973) 'Abstracting as a fine art', *Information Scientist*, 7(2): 43–53.

Aslib (2008) *Abstracting and Summarising Quickly and Accurately*. Accessed on 6 August 2008 online at: *http:// www.aslib.co.uk/training/4/01.html.* (Training programme available online at: *http://www.aslib.co.uk/training/4/ Abstracting.pdf.*)

Attfield, S., Blandford, A. and Dowell, J. (2003) 'Information seeking in the context of writing: a design psychology interpretation of the "problematic situation"', *Journal of Documentation*, 59(4): 430–53.

Aucamp, P.J. (1980) 'The science of abstracting – a précis', *South African Libraries*, 48(1): 25–8.

Ayers, G. (2008) 'The evolutionary nature of genre: an investigation of the short texts accompanying research articles in the scientific journal *Nature*', *English for Specific Purposes*, 27(1): 22–41.

Bańczerowski, J. (2000a) 'Metainformációs struktúrák a nyelvi szöveg síkján', in István Nyomárkay (szerk.), *A nyelv és a nyelvi kommunikáció alapkérdései*. Budapest: ELTE, pp. 132–43.

Bańczerowski, J. (2000b) 'A kommunikációs kompetencia és összetevői', in István Nyomárkay (szerk.), *A nyelv és a nyelvi kommunikáció alapkérdései*. Budapest: ELTE, pp. 342–51.

Bańczerowski, J. (2000c) 'A transzlatorika fogalmának meghatározásához', in István Nyomárkay (szerk.), *A nyelv és a nyelvi kommunikáció alapkérdései*. Budapest: ELTE, pp. 392–6.

Bawden, D. (2001) 'Information and digital literacies: a review of concepts', *Journal of Documentation*, 57(2): 218–59.

Bawden, D. et al. (2007) 'Towards Curriculum 2.0: library/information education for a Web 2.0 world', *Library and Information Research*, 31(99). Accessed on 20 December 2008 online at: *http://www.lirg.org.uk/lir/ojs/index.php/lir/article/view/49/74*.

Beeson, I. (2005) 'Judging relevance: a problem for e-literacy', *ITALICS*, 4(2). Accessed on 20 December 2008 online at: *http://www.ics.headacademy.ac.uk/italics/vol5iss4/beeson.pdf*.

Beghtol, C. (1986) 'Bibliographic classification theory and text linguistics: aboutness analysis, intertextuality and the cognitive art of classifying documents', *Journal of Documentation*, 42(2), 84–133.

Belkin, N.J. (1993) 'On the relationship between discourse structure and user intention', *Summarizing Text for Intelligent Communication*. Accessed on 26 June 2008 online at: *http://www.ik.fh-hannover.de/ik/projekte/ Dagstuhl/Abstract/Abstracts/Belkin/Belkin.html.*

Berkenkotter, C. and Huckin, T (1995) *Genre Knowledge in Disciplinary Communication.* Hillsdale, NJ: Erlbaum.

Black, W.J. (1990) 'Knowledge-based abstracting', *Online Review*, 14(5): 327–40.

Boekhorst, A. (2003) 'Becoming information literate in the Netherlands', *Library Review*, 52(7): 298–309.

Borko, H. and Bernier, C.L. (1975) *Abstracting Concepts and Methods.* New York: Academic Press.

Busch-Lauer, I.A. (1995) 'Abstracts in German medical journals: a linguistic analysis', *Information Processing and Management*, 31(5): 769–76.

Cain, E.B. (1988) *The Basics of Technical Communicating.* Washington, DC: American Chemical Society.

Carraway, L. (2007) 'Content and organization of a scientific paper', *American Midland Naturalist*, 157(2): 412–22.

Chan, S.K. and Foo, S. (2001) 'Bridging the interdisciplinary gap in abstract writing for scholarly communication', in *Genres and Discourse in Education, Work and Cultural Life.* Oslo: Oslo University College.

Chan, S.K. and Foo, S. (2004) 'Interdisciplinary perspectives on abstracts for information retrieval', *Ibérica*, 8: 100–24. Accessed on 22 August 2008 online at: *http://www.aelfe.org/documents/07-RA-8-Chan-Foo.pdf.*

Chuah, K. (2001) *Types of Lexical Substitution in Abstracting.* Proceedings of the ACL-2001 Student Research Workshop, Toulouse. Accessed on 22 August 2008 online at: *https://nats-www.informatik.uni-hamburg .de/intern/proceedings/2001/acl-eacl/student/chuah.pdf.*

CILIP (Chartered Institute of Library and Information Professionals) (2004) *A Short Introduction to Information Literacy.* Accessed on 3 October 2007 online at: *http://www.cilip.org.uk/professionalguidance/ informationliteracy/definition/introduction.htm.*

Clayton, J. (2006) 'Writing an executive summary that means business', in *Written Communications that Inform and Influence.* Boston: Harvard Business School Press, pp. 145–9.

Cleveland, D.B. and Cleveland, A.D. (1983) *Introduction to Indexing and Abstracting.* Littleton, CO: Libraries Unlimited.

Collison, R.L. (1971) *Abstracts and Abstracting Services.* Santa Barbara, CA: ABC Clio.

'Competence' (2008) See *Wikipedia.* Accessed on 4 March 2009 online at: *http://en.wikipedia.org/wiki/Competence.*

Connor, U. and Mauranen, A. (1999) 'Linguistic analysis of grant proposals: European Union research grants', *English for Specific Purposes,* 18(1): 47–62.

Craven, T.C. (1993) 'A computer-aided abstracting tool kit', *Canadian Journal of Information and Library Science,* 18(2): 20–31.

Crawford, W. (2009) 'Futurism and Librarie', *Online,* 33(2): 58-60.

Cremmins, E.T. (1982) *The Art of Abstracting.* Philadelphia, PA: ISI Press.

Cross, C. and Oppenheim, C. (2006) 'A genre analysis of scientific abstracts', *Journal of Documentation,* 62(4): 428–46.

Cummings, P. (2004) 'Writing informative abstracts for journal articles', *Archives of Pediatrics and Adolescent Medicine,* 158(11): 1086–8.

Curtis, D. and Bernhardt, S.A. (1992) 'Keywords, titles, abstracts and online searches: implications for technical writing', *Technical Writing Teacher,* 18(2): 142–61.

D'Angelo, B.J. and Maid, B.M. (2004) 'Moving beyond definitions: implementing information literacy across the curriculum', *Journal of Academic Librarianship*, 30(3): 212–17.

Dashkin, M. (2003) 'Electronic writing: defining a core competency', *Information Outlook*, 7(9): 34–7.

Day, R.A. (1988) *How to Write and Publish a Scientific Paper*, 3rd edn. Phoenix, AZ: Oryx.

De Beaugrande, R.A. and Dressler, W. (2002) *Introduction to Text Linguistics*. Accessed on 20 March 2009 online at: *http://www.beaugrande.com/introduction_to_text_linguistics.htm*.

De Guire, E. (2006) 'Publish or perish: afterlife of a published article'. Accessed on 11 August 2009 online at: *http://www.csa.com/discoveryguides/publish/review.php*.

December, J. and Katz, S. (1991) *Abstracts*. Accessed on 11 August 2009 online at: *http://www.rpi.edu/web/writingcenter/abstracts.html*.

'Deep structure' (2009) See *Encyclopaedia Britannica Online*. Accessed on 11 March 2009 online at: *http://www.britannica.com/EBchecked/topic/155528/deep-structure*.

EBSCO (2008) *EBSCO Infoday*. PowerPoint Presentation. Accessed on 26 July 2008 online at: *http://www.ki.oszk.hu/107/e107_files/downloads/bolcsesztudomanyiadatb_1resz.pdf*.

Eisenberg, M. (2007) *A Big6 Skills Overview*. Accessed on 20 December 2008 online at: *http://www.big6.com/category/overview-of-big6-skills/*.

Elmborg, J.K. (2003) 'Information literacy and writing across the curriculum: sharing the vision', *Reference Services Review*, 31(1): 68–80.

Elmborg, J.K. (2006) 'Critical information literacy: implications for instructional practice', *Journal of Academic Librarianship*, 32(2): 192–9.

Emashova, O.A. (2008) 'An approach to the automatic abstracting of Russian texts', *Moscow University Computational Mathematics and Cybernetics*, 32(1): 54–9.

Endres-Niggemeyer, B. (1989) Content analysis – a special case of text compression', in *Information, Knowledge, Evolution*. Amsterdam: Elsevier, pp. 103–12.

Endres-Niggemeyer, B. (1990) 'A procedural model of an abstractor at work', *International Forum on Information and Documentation*, 15(4): 3–15.

Endres-Niggemeyer, B. (1998) *Summarizing Information*. Berlin: Springer.

Endres-Niggemeyer, B. (2000) *Human-style WWW Summarization*. Hannover: University of Applied Sciences and Arts. Accessed on 20 December 2008 online at: *http://summit-bmt.fh-hannover.de/papers/pdf/Human-styleSummaNew.pdf*.

Endres-Niggemeyer, B. and Neugebauer, E. (1998) 'Professional summarizing: no cognitive simulation without observation', *Journal of the American Society for Information Science*, 49(6): 486–506.

Endres-Niggemeyer, B., Maier, E. and Sigel, A. (1995) 'How to implement a naturalistic model of abstracting: four core working steps of an expert abstractor', *Information Processing and Management*, 31(5): 631–74.

ETA (2006) *Knowledge Skills and Abilities*. Employment and Training Administration of the United States Department of Labor. Accessed on 4 March 2009 online at: *http://www.doleta.gov/jobs/Federal_Application_Process/Knowledge_Skills_Abilities/*.

Farrow, J.F. (1991) 'A cognitive model of document indexing', *Journal of Documentation*, 47(2): 149–66.

Fattahi, R. (1998) 'Library cataloging and abstracting and indexing services: reconciliation of principles in the online environment?', *Library Review*, 47(4): 211–16.

Fidel, R. (1986) 'The possible effect of abstracting guidelines on retrieval performance of free-text searching', *Information Processing and Management*, 22(4): 309–16.

Fidel, R. (1993) 'User-centered text analysis', *Summarizing Text for Intelligent Communication*. Accessed on 26 June 2008 online at: *http://www.ik.fh-hannover.de/ik/projekte/ Dagstuhl/Abstract/Abstracts/Fidel/Fidel.html*.

Fitzgibbons, M. (2008) 'Implications of hypertext theory for the reading, organization, and retrieval of information', *Library Philosophy and Practice*. Accessed on 26 July 2008 online at: *http://www.webpages.uidaho.edu/~ mbolin/fitzgibbons.htm*.

Friedrich, H.F. (1993) 'Training of reductive text learning strategies', *Summarizing Text for Intelligent Communication*. Accessed on 26 June 2008 online at: *http://www.ik.fh-hannover.de/ik/projekte/Dagstuhl/ Abstract/Abstracts/Friedrich/Friedrich.html*.

Garner, R. (1982) 'Efficient text summarization: costs and benefits', *Journal of Educational Research*, 75 (5): 275–9.

Gläser, R. (1993) 'Summarizing texts as genres of academic writing', *Summarizing Text for Intelligent Communication*. Accessed on 26 June 2008 online at: *http://www.ik.fh-hannover.de/ik/projekte/Dagstuhl/Abstract/ Abstracts/Glaeser/Glaeser.html*.

Goldbort, R. (2002) 'Abstracts for scientific articles', *Journal of Environmental Health*, 65(4): 26–7.

Granville, S. and Dison, L. (2005) 'Thinking about thinking: integrating self-reflection into an academic literacy course', *Journal of English for Academic Purposes*, 4(2): 99–118.

Guide for Reviewers (2008) *Mathematical Reviews Database*. Accessed on 6 August 2008 online at: *http://www.ams.org/authors/guide-reviewers.html*.

Guinn, D.M. (1979) 'Composing an abstract: a practical heuristic', *College Composition and Communication*, 30(4): 380–3.

Hall, D.M. (1986) 'Writing abstracts: the American National Standard', *Bulletin of the American Society for Information Science*, 13(1): 35.

Hartley, J. (2004) 'Current findings from research on structured abstracts', *Journal of the Medical Library Association*, 92(3): 368–71.

Hartley, J., Pennebacker, J.W. and Fox, C. (2003) 'Abstracts, introductions and discussions: how far do they differ in style?', *Scientometrics*, 57(3): 389–98.

Hartley, J., Branthwaite, A., Ganier, F. and Heurley, L. (2007) 'Lost in translation: contributions of editors to the meanings of text', *Journal of Information Science*, 33(5): 551–65.

Hartley, J. et al. (2003) 'Improving the clarity of journal abstracts in psychology: the case for structure', *Science Communication*, 24(3): 366–79.

Hawkins, D.T. and Brynko, B. (2008) 'NFAIS: the next 50 years', *Information Today*, 25(4): 1–5.

Haynes, R.B. et al. (1990) 'More informative abstracts revisited', *Annals of Internal Medicine*, 113(1): 69–76.

Hjørland, B. (2000) 'Library and information science; practice, theory, and philosophical basis', *Information Processing and Management*, 36(3): 501–31.

Houp, K.W. and Pearsall, T.E. (1988) *Reporting Technical Information*. New York: Macmillan.

Hughes, W. (2006) *How to Write Informative Abstracts*. Accessed on 7 October 2008 online at: *http://www.personal .rdg.ac.uk/~kcshuwil/cme/abstract.html*.

Hutchins, W.J. (1977) 'On the problem of "aboutness" in document analysis', *Journal of Informatics*, 1(1): 17–35.

Hutchins, W.J. (1983) 'Some problems and methods of text condensation', *UEA Papers in Linguistics*, 19: 38–54. Accessed on 17 April 2008 online at: *http://www .hutchinsweb.me.uk/UEAPIL-1983.pdf*.

Hutchins, W.J. (1987) 'Summarization: some problems and methods', *Meaning: The Frontier of Informatics. Informatics 9*. London: Aslib, pp. 151–73.

Hutchins, W.J. (1993) 'Introduction to "Text Summarization" workshop', *Summarizing Text for Intelligent Communication*. Accessed on 17 April 2008 online at: *http://www.hutchinsweb.me.uk/Dagstuhl-1993.pdf*.

Hyland, K. (2007) 'Genre pedagogy: language, literacy and L2 writing instruction', *Journal of Second Language Writing*, 16(3): 148–64.

Iatsko, V. (2001) 'Linguistic aspects of summarization', *PhiN. Philologie im Netz*, 18: 33–46. Accessed on 16 March 2009 online at: *http://web.fu-berlin.de/phin/phin18/p18i.htm*.

International Committee of Medical Journal Editors (1982) 'Uniform requirements for manuscripts submitted to biomedical journals', *British Medical Journal*, 284: 1766–70. See also at: *http://www.icmje.org/index.html* (accessed on 25 July 2008).

Jacsó, P. (2002) 'Document-summarization software', *Information Today*, 19(2): 22–3.

Jacsó, P. (2006) 'Open access to scholarly indexing/abstracting information', *Online Information Review*, 30(4): 461–8.

Johnson, F. (1995) 'Automatic abstracting research', *Library Review*, 44(8): 28–36.

Johnston, B. and Webber, S. (2003) 'Information literacy in higher education: a review and case study', *Studies in Higher Education*, 28(3): 335–52.

Jones, D. (1996) *Critical Thinking in an Online World*. Accessed on 21 April 2008 online at: *http://www.library.ucsb.edu/untangle/jones.html*.

Karasev, S.A. (1978) 'Referirovania nauchno-tekhnicheskoi literatury: elementy teorii', *Nauchno-Tekhnicheskaya Informatsiya*, Series 2 (10): 1–4.

Kilborn, J. (1998) *Writing Abstracts*. Accessed on 20 December 2008 online at: *http://leo.stcloudstate.edu/bizwrite/abstracts.html*.

Kintsch, W. and van Dijk, T. (1983) *Strategies of Discourse Comprehension*. Ireland, FL: Academic Press.

Kittredge, R. (2002) 'Paraphrasing for condensation in journal abstracting', *Journal of Biomedical Informatics*, 35(4): 265–77.

Klaudy, K. (1979) 'Fordítás és aktuális tagolás', *Magyar Nyelvőr*, 103(4): 282–7.

Koltay, T. (1997a) 'A wider horizon to information handling: teaching abstracting to students of translation', *Education for Information*, 15(1): 35–42.

Koltay, T. (1997b) 'The role of abstracting in "professional documentation", a technical writing class for Hungarian students of English translation', *Journal of Technical Writing and Communication*, 27(3): 277–89.

Koltay, T. (1998) 'Including technical and academic writing in translation curricula', *Translation Journal*, 2(2). Accessed on 20 December 2008 online at: *http://accurapid.com/journal/04educ.htm*.

Koltay, T. (1999) Writing globally: teaching technical writing to Hungarian students of translation', *Journal of Business and Technical Communication*, 13(1): 86–93.

Koltay, T. (2002) 'Teaching proposal writing to translators', *Translation Journal*, 6(2). Accessed on 20 December 2008 online at: *http://www.accurapid.com/journal/20edu.htm*.

Koltay, T. (2003) *A referálás elmélete és gyakorlata*. Budapest: Könyvtári Intézet.

Koopman, P. (1997) *How to Write an Abstract*. Accessed on 6 August 2008 online at: *http://www.ece.cmu.edu/~koopman/essays/abstract.html*.

Kuhlen, R. (1984) 'Some similarities and differences between intellectual and machine text understanding for the purpose of abstracting', in *Representation and*

Exchange of Knowledge as a Basis of Information Processes. Amsterdam: Elsevier.

Kwan, B. (2008) 'The nexus of reading, writing and researching in the doctoral undertaking of humanities and social sciences: implications for literature reviewing', *English for Specific Purposes*, 27(1): 42–56.

Laflen, A. (2001) *Understanding the Sections of Your Report. Abstract*. Accessed on 22 August 2008 online at: *http://owl.english.purdue.edu/workshops/hypertext/reportW/abstract.html*.

Lancaster, F.W. (1991) *Indexing and Abstracting in Theory and Practice*. Champaign, IL: Graduate School of Library and Information Science.

Lancaster, F.W. (2003) 'Do indexing and abstracting have a future?', *Anales de Documentación*, 6: 137–44.

Lannon, J.M. (1990) *Technical Writing*, 5th edn. Boston: Little, Brown.

Leonardi, V. (2000) 'Equivalence in translation: between myth and reality', *Translation Journal*, 4(4). Accessed on 22 February 2009 online at: *http://accurapid.com/journal/14equiv.htm*.

Locker, K.O. (1982) 'Teaching students to write abstracts', *Technical Writing Teacher*, 10(1): 17–20.

Loo, A. and Chung, C.W. (2006) 'A model for information literacy course development: a liberal arts university perspective', *Library Review*, 55(4): 249–58.

Lorés, R. (2004) 'On RA abstracts: from rhetorical structure to thematic organisation', *English for Specific Purposes*, 23(3): 280–302.

Lynch, C. (1998) *Information Literacy and Information Technology Literacy: New Components in the Curriculum for a Digital Culture*. Accessed on 21 April 2008 online at: *http://www.cni.org/staff/cliffpubs/info_and_IT_literacy.pdf*.

McKeown, K.R., Robin, J. and Kukich, K. (1995) 'Generating concise natural language summaries', *Information Processing and Management*, 31(5): 703–33.

Magnet, A. and Carnet, D. (2006) Letters to the editor: 'Still vigorous after all these years? A presentation of the discursive and linguistic features of the genre', *English for Specific Purposes*, 25(2): 173–99.

Maizell, R.E., Smith, J.F. and Singer, T.E.R. (1971) *Abstracting Scientific and Technical Literature: An Introductory Guide and Text for Abstractors and Management*. New York: Wiley Interscience.

Manion, Ch. (2008) *Abstracting*. Accessed on 6 August 2008 online at: *http://people.cohums.ohio-state.edu/manion12/classdocs/abstracting.htm*.

Manning, A.D. (1990) 'Abstracts in relation to larger and smaller discourse structures', *Journal of Technical Writing and Communication*, 20(4): 369–90.

Martín Martín, P. (2003) 'A genre analysis of English and Spanish research paper abstracts in experimental social sciences', *English for Specific Purposes*, 22(1): 25–43.

Mathematical Reviews (2008) See *Wikipedia*. Accessed on 6 August 2008 online at: *http://en.wikipedia.org/wiki/Mathematical_Reviews*.

Mathis, B.A. and Rush, J.E. (1975) 'Abstracting', in J. Belzer (ed.), *Encyclopedia of Computer Science and Technology*. New York: Marcel Dekker, pp. 102–42.

Montesi, M. and Urdiciain, B.G. (2005a) 'Recent linguistic research into author abstracts: its value for information science', *Knowledge Organization*, 32(2): 64–78.

Montesi, M. and Urdiciain, B.G. (2005b) 'Abstracts: problems classified from the user perspective', *Journal of Information Science*, 31(6): 515–26.

Murray, D. (1980) *Learning by Teaching: Selected Articles on Writing and Teaching*. Portsmouth, NJ: Boynton-Cook. Cited by Kwan (2008).

Nakayama, T., Hirai, N., Yamazaki, S. and Naito, M. (2005) 'Adoption of structured abstracts by general medical journals and format for a structured abstract', *Journal of the Medical Library Association*, 93(2): 237–42.

Neal, D. (2007) 'Introduction. Folksonomies and image tagging: seeing the future?', *Bulletin of the American Society for Information Science and Technology*, (34)1: 7–11. Accessed on 21 December 2008 online at: *http://www.asis.org/Bulletin/Oct-07/Neal_OctNov07.pdf*.

Neufeld, M.L. and Cornog, M. (1983) *Abstracting and Indexing: A Career Guide*. Philadelphia, PA: NFAIS.

Nicholas, D., Huntington, P. and Jamali, H.R. (2007) 'The use, users, and role of abstracts in the digital scholarly environment', *Journal of Academic Librarianship*, 33(4): 446–53.

Nohr, H. (1999) 'Inhaltsanalyse', *Nachrichten für Dokumentation*, 50(2): 69–73.

Novikov, A.I. and Nesterova, N.M. (1991) *Referativnyj perevod nauchno-tekhnicheskich tekstov*. Moskva.

Nwogu, K.N. (1995) 'Structuring scientific discourse using the "given-new" perspective', *English Teaching Forum*, 33(4). Accessed on 24 April 2009 online at: *http://eca.state.gov/forum/vols/vol33/NO4/p22.htm*.

Orasan, C. and Hasler, L. (2006) 'Computer-aided summarisation – what the user really wants', in *Proceedings of LREC 2006*, Genoa, Italy. Accessed on 27 June 2008 online at: *http://www.sdjt.si/bib/lrec06/*.

Palais, E.S. (1988) 'Abstracting for reference librarians', *Reference Librarian*, 9(22): 297–308.

Paul, R. (1993) *Critical Thinking: What Every Person Needs to Survive in a Rapidly Changing World*. Santa Rosa, CA: Foundation for Critical Thinking.

Pfeiffer-Jäger, G. (1980) 'Referat und Referieren', *Germanistische Linguistik*, 1–2: 1–180.

Pho, P.D. (2008) 'Research article abstracts in applied linguistics and educational technology: a study of linguistic realizations of rhetorical structure and authorial stance', *Discourse Studies*, 10(2): 231–50.

Pinto, M. (1992) *El resúmen documental. Pricípios y métodos*. Madrid: Fundación Germán Sánchez Ruipérez.

Pinto, M. (1994) 'Interdisciplinary approaches to the concept and practice of written text documentary content analysis (WTDCA)', *Journal of Documentation*, 50(2): 111–33.

Pinto, M. (1995) 'Documentary abstracting: toward a methodological model', *Journal of the American Society for Information Science*, 46(3): 225–34.

Pinto, M. (2003a) 'Engineering the production of meta-information: the abstracting concern', *Journal of Information Science*, 29(5): 405–17.

Pinto, M. (2003b) 'Abstracting/abstract adaptation to digital environments: research trends', *Journal of Documentation*, 59(5): 581–608.

Pinto, M. (2006a) 'Data representation factors and dimensions from the quality function deployment (QFD) perspective', *Journal of Information Science*, 32(2): 116–30.

Pinto, M. (2006b) 'A grounded theory on abstract quality: weighting variables and attributes', *Scientometrics*, 69(2): 213–26.

Pinto, M. (2008) 'Cyberabstracts: a portal on the subject of abstracting designed to improve information literacy skills', *Journal of Information Science*, 20(10): 1–13.

Pinto, M. and Gálvez, C. (1999) 'Paradigms for abstracting systems', *Journal of Information Science*, 25(5): 365–80.

Pinto, M. and Lancaster, F.W. (1999) 'Abstracts and abstracting in knowledge discovery', *Library Trends*, 48(1): 234–48.

Pinto, M. and Sales, D. (2007) 'A research case study for user-centred information literacy instruction: information behaviour of translation trainees', *Journal of Information Science*, 33(5): 531–50.

Pinto, M., Fernández-Ramos, A. and Doucet, A.-V. (2008a) 'Measuring students' information literacy skills through abstracting: case study from a library and information science perspective', *College and Research Libraries*, 69(2): 132–54.

Pinto, M., Fernández-Ramos, A. and Doucet, A.-V. (2008b) 'The role of information competencies and skills in learning to abstract', *Journal of Information Science*, 34(6): 799–815.

Pinto, M. et al. (2005) *Aprendiendo a resumir: prontuario y resolución de casos*. Gijón: Trea.

Pitkin, R.M. and Branagan, M.N. (1998) 'Can the accuracy of abstracts be improved by providing specific instructions? A randomized controlled trial', *Journal of the American Medical Association*, 280(3): 267–9.

Pitkin, R.M., Branagan, M.A. and Burmeister, L.F. (1999) 'Accuracy of data in abstracts of published research articles', *Journal of the American Medical Association*, 281(12): 1110–11.

Polzovics, I. (1962) *Bevezetés a szakirodalmi dokumentációba a műszaki és természettudományok terén*. Budapest: OMKDK.

Posteguillo, S. (1999) 'The schematic structure of computer science research articles', *English for Specific Purposes*, 18(2): 139–58.

Procter, M. (2008) *The Abstract*. Accessed on 26 June 2008 online at: *http://www.utoronto.ca/writing/abstract.html*.

Radzievskaya, T.V. (1986) 'Referativnyi tekst v lingvopragmaticheskom aspekte', *Nauchno-Tekhnicheskaya Informatsiya*, Series 2(8): 1–5.

Rathbone, R. (1972) *Communicating Technical Information*. Reading, MA: Addison Wesley.

Roberts, D. (1982) 'Teaching abstracts in technical writing: early and often', *Technical Writing Teacher*, 10: 112–16.

Roes, H. (2001) 'Digital libraries and education: trends and opportunities', *D-Lib Magazine*, 7(7–8). Accessed on 12 January 2009 online at: *http://www.dlib.org/dlib/july01/roes/07roes.html*.

Root-Bernstein, R.S. (1991) 'Teaching abstracting in an integrated art and science curriculum', *Roeper Review*, 13(2): 85–90.

Rosen, B.C. (1988) 'The age of the information broker: an introduction', *Reference Librarian*, 22(1): 5–16.

Rosso, M.A. (2008) 'Stalking the Wild Web Genre (with apologies to Euell Gibbons)', *Bulletin of the American Society for Information Science and Technology*, 34(5): 20–2. Accessed on 17 August 2008 online at: *http://www.asis.org/Bulletin/Jun-08/JunJul08_Rosso.pdf*.

Rothkegel, A. (1995) 'Abstracting from the perspective of text production', *Information Processing and Management*, 31(5): 777–84.

Roundy, N. (1982) 'A process approach to teaching the abstract', *ABCA Bulletin*, 45(3): 34–8.

Rowlett, R.J. (1985) 'Abstracts and other information filters', *Journal of Chemical Information and Computer Sciences*, 25(3): 159–63.

Rowley, J. (1988) *Abstracting and Indexing*, 2nd edn. London: Clive Bingley.

Rulewicz, W. (1995) 'A grammar of narrativity: Algirdas Julien Greimas', *Glasgow Review*, 3. Accessed on 11 March 2009 online at: *http://www.arts.gla.ac.uk/SESLL/STELLA/COMET/glasgrev/issue3/rudz.htm*.

Russel, P. (1988) *How to Write a Précis*. Ottawa: University of Ottawa Press.

Saggion, H. (1999) 'Using linguistic knowledge in automatic abstracting', *Proceedings of the 37th Annual Meeting of the Association for Computational Linguistics*. Accessed on 9 August 2008 online at: *http://www.aclweb.org/anthology-new/P/P99/P99-1078.pdf*.

Salager-Meyer, F. (1991) 'Medical English abstracts: how well are they structured?', *Journal of the American Society of Information Science*, 42(7): 528–31.

Samraj, B. (2005) 'An exploration of a genre set: research article abstracts and introductions in two disciplines', *English for Specific Purposes*, 24(2): 141–56.

Sherrard, C.A. (1985) 'The psychology of summary-writing', *Journal of Technical Writing and Communication*, 15(3): 247–58.

Sidorov, E.V. (1982) 'Kharakteristike teksta kak podsistemy (v obychnoj kommunikacii i v kommunikacii s referirovaniem)', *Prevod kak lingisticheskaya problema*. Moskva: MGU, pp. 12–27.

Siebers, R. (2001) 'Data inconsistencies in abstracts of articles in clinical chemistry', *Clinical Chemistry*, 47(1): 149.

SIL International (2004) 'What is a proposition?' Accessed on 25 March 2009 online at: *http://www2.sil.org/linguistics/GlossaryOfLinguisticTerms/WhatIsAProposition.htm*.

Slade, C. (1997) *Form and Style: Research Papers, Reports, Theses*, 10th edn. Boston: Houghton Mifflin.

Sparck Jones, K. (1993) 'Summarising: analytic framework, key component, experimental method', *Summarizing Text for Intelligent Communication*. Accessed on 26 June 2008 online at: *http://www.ik.fh-hannover.de/ik/projekte/Dagstuhl/Abstract/Abstracts/Sparck/Sparck.html*.

Staiger, D. (1965) 'What today's students need to know about writing abstracts', *Journal of Business Communication*, 3(1): 29–33.

Steinerová, J. and Šušol, J. (2007) 'Users' information behaviour – a gender perspective', *Information Research*,

12(3): paper 320. Accessed on 29 June 2008 online at: *http://InformationR.net/ir/12-3/paper320.html*.

Stotesbury, H. (2003) 'Evaluation in research article abstracts in the narrative and hard sciences', *Journal of English for Academic Purposes*, 2(4): 327–41.

Swales, J.M. (1990) *Genre Analysis: English in Academic and Research Settings*. Cambridge: Cambridge University Press.

Taylor, R.S. (1984) 'Value-added processes in document-based systems: abstracting and indexing services', *Information Services and Use*, 4(3): 127–46.

Tenopir, C. (2008) 'Online databases: new order, new thinking', *Library Journal*, 133. Accessed on 6 April 2009 online at: *http://www.libraryjournal.com/article/CA6551205.html*.

Tenopir, C. and Jacsó, P. (1993) 'Quality of abstracts', *Online*, 17(3): 44, 46–8, 50–5.

Thistlethwaite, L.L. (1991) 'Summarizing: it's more than just finding the main idea. A six-phase plan for teaching summarization', *Intervention in School and Clinic*, 27 (1): 25–30.

Tibbo, H.R. (1992) 'Abstracting across the disciplines: a content analysis of abstracts from the natural sciences, the social sciences, and the humanities with implications for abstracting standards and online information retrieval', *Library and Information Science Research*, 14(1): 31–56.

Tibbo, H.R. (1994a) 'Abstracting, information retrieval and the humanities: providing access to historical literature', *Journal of Librarianship and Information Science*, 26(1): 39–40.

Tibbo, H.R. (1994b) 'Indexing for the humanities', *Journal of the American Society for Information Science*, 45(8): 607–19.

Trawinski, B. (1989) 'A methodology for writing problem structured abstracts', *Information Processing and Management*, 25(6): 693–702.

Turner, A. (2003) *Abstract Writing*. Accessed on 26 June 2008 online at: *http://ctl.hanyang.ac.kr:8001/writing/research_article/abstract.htm*.

UNESCO (1988) *Proposed International Standard Nomenclature for Fields of Science and Technology*. Paris. Accessed on 26 June 2008 online at: *http://unesdoc.unesco.org/images/0008/000829/082946EB.pdf*.

Uso, E. and Palmer, J.C. (1998) 'A product-focused approach to text summarisation', *Internet TESL Journal*, 4(1). Accessed on 2 March 2009 online at: *http://iteslj.org/Articles/Juan-TextSummary.html*.

Van Dijk, T. (1980) *Macrostructures*. Hillsdale, NJ: Erlbaum.

Van Dijk, T. (1996) 'Prólogo', in M. Pinto and C. Gálvez (eds), *Análisis documental de contenido*. Madrid: Síntesis, pp. 9–11.

Van Dijk, T. (2005) 'Macrostructure', *TEXTOPEDIA – Discurso y Sociedad*. Accessed on 26 June 2008 online at: *http://www.dissoc.org/proyectos/textopedia/Textopedia-Macrostructure.html*.

Vaughan, D.K. (1991) 'Abstracts and summaries: some clarifying distinctions', *Technical Writing Teacher*, 18(2): 132–41.

Ward, D. (2006) 'Revisioning information literacy for lifelong learning', *Journal of Academic Librarianship*, 32(4): 396–402.

Waters, M. (1982) 'Abstracts – an overlooked management writing skill', *ABCA Bulletin*, 45(2): 219–21.

Wenden, A. (1999) 'An introduction to metacognitive knowledge and beliefs in language learning: beyond the basics', *System*, 27(4): 435–41.

Werlich, E. (1988) *Student's Guide to Text Production*. Berlin: Cornelsen.

Widdowson, H. (1979) 'The process and purpose of reading', *Explorations in Applied Linguistics*. New York: Oxford University Press, pp. 171–83.

Winker, M.A. (1999) 'The need for concrete improvement in abstract quality', *Journal of the American Medical Association*, 281(12): 1129–30.

Wolf, S. (2007) 'Information literacy and self-regulation: a convergence of disciplines', *School Library Media Research*, 10. Accessed on 5 July 2008 online at: *http://www.ala.org/ala/aasl/aaslpubsandjournals/slmrb/slmrcontents/volume10/wolf_informationliteracy.cfm*.

Yu, G. (2009) 'The shifting sands in the effects of source text summarizability on summary writing', *Assessing Writing*, 14(2): 116–37.

Zellers, K. et al. (2008) *Writing Abstracts*. Colorado State University Department of English. Accessed on 6 April 2009 online at: *http://writing.colostate.edu/guides/documents/abstract/*.

Index

Printed in Great Britain
by Amazon

39195287R00132